BRITISH INFANTRYMAN

The British and Commonwealth soldier 1939–45 (all models)

First published in November 2020

A catalogue record for this book is available from the British Library.

ISBN 978 1 78521 720 3

Library of Congress control no. 2020932128

Published by J H Haynes & Co. Ltd.,
Sparkford, Yeovil, Somerset BA22 7JJ, UK.
Tel: 01963 440635
Int. tel: +44 1963 440635
Website: www.haynes.com

Haynes North America Inc.,
859 Lawrence Drive, Newbury Park,
California 91320, USA.

Printed in Malaysia.

Senior Commissioning Editor: Jonathan Falconer
Copy editor: Michelle Tilling
Proof reader: Penny Housden
Indexer: Peter Nicholson
Page design: James Robertson

Acknowledgements

This book would not have been produced without the material help of a number of people. Thanks to my brothers – Jonathan for material on uniforms and equipment and Adam for access to the library of the Royal Signals Museum at Blandford Forum and help with the signals section. Thanks also to Tom Moncur for checking the RCS section; Elly for some badges; Mark Franklin for the maps; Richard Charlton-Taylor for weapons and tactics and pointing out other useful things; Ed Hallett for his help with uniform captioning; Tim and Preston Isaac at the unbeatable Cobbaton Combat Collection; and Dr Patrick Hook for vehicles. The photographs come from a variety of sources. Most of the wartime photographs are from NARA, College Park, USA, the Library and Archives, Canada, the Battlefield Historian military archive (thanks Neil), the National Archive of the Netherlands, and the collections of official material provided by the late Martin Warren and my late father. The modern photographs come from photo shoots with the excellent East Yorks Re-enactment Group: thanks in particular to Dave Hebden, who set it up, and Gary Hancock, who hosted it and helped with the proof reading. Other material comes from Richard Charlton-Taylor, Greene Media (thanks Alan!), Ed Hallett, Patrick Hook, the Royal Signals Museum, Alec Small and his wonderful collection of vehicles (including bicycles), Aline Staes at York Army Museum, and Christopher Williams of RPJ Militaria who provided images of more Second World War original cloth badges than I knew existed.

Thanks, too, to Sandra for reading it and asking difficult questions. The project was managed by the excellent Jonathan Falconer of Haynes and thanks to editor Michelle Tilling for significant improvements and designer James Robertson for making a quart fit into a pint pot.

BRITISH INFANTRYMAN

The British and Commonwealth soldier 1939–45 (all models)

Operations Manual

An insight into the weapons, uniform, accoutrements, equipment and tactics of the Second World War British infantryman

Simon Forty

Contents

OPPOSITE The best laid plans ... Operation Veritable – clearing the Rhineland – was supposed to take place on winter-hardened ground. Instead, the aftermath of the battle of the Bulge saw the operation delayed until February by which time a thaw had set in. This, compounded by the breaching of the Roer dams, meant British and Canadian troops had to fight their way, inch by muddy inch, through the Reichswald and the floods.

Preface

──●──

The rifleman fights without promise of either reward or relief. Behind every river there's another hill and behind that hill, another river. After weeks or months in the line only a wound can offer him the comfort of safety, shelter and a bed. Those who are left fight on, evading death but knowing that with each day of evasion they have exhausted one more chance for survival. Sooner or later, unless victory comes this chase must end on a litter or in a grave.

General Omar N. Bradley

OPPOSITE The conscript armies of the Western Allies have had a bad press, but victory in North Africa netted 250,000 prisoners and set them on the path to victory in Europe – with the British infantrymen playing a significant part. These men are seen in Bizerte on 8 May 1943. The leading man carries a Thompson SMG, the others a Lee-Enfield SMLE, then another Thompson, next a Bren and, finally, another Lee-Enfield. *(All photos from author's collection except where credited otherwise)*

BELOW General
Bernard L. Montgomery
talks to paras of 6th
Airborne Division in
March 1944. Postwar
nationalist leanings
have tended to malign
him and his troops'
showing in Normandy.
In fact British and
Canadian troops
performed magnificently
against the weight of
German armour.

The British infantryman had a bad press in the latter part of the 20th century. Apart from the regular accusations of poor equipment, poor generals, poor tactics, dependence on artillery, inability to fight with tanks, the superiority of German and Japanese infantry and – most damning – their propensity to brew up when they should have been advancing, the British have regularly been the butt of disparaging comments from populist historians on both sides of the Atlantic.

The reality is, of course, completely different. All armies are a mixture of good and bad: the Germans may have had a brilliant training system, excellent NCOs and introduced Blitzkrieg to the world, but they used more horses than lorries, shot over 40,000 soldiers for desertion and other crimes, coerced the others through the concept of kin liability – *Sippenhaft*, that allowed the Nazis to take out their frustrations on the families of soldiers they decided hadn't done their duty – and all the time their generals were the pawns of a dictator whose decision-making seemed increasingly unhinged. Their vaunted Atlantic Wall lasted less than 24 hours when attacked by the same soldiers whose prowess is derided. On the other hand, with Hollywood at the fore, the

Americans point to the success of Operation Cobra, Patton's exploitation of First Army's breakthough, the defeat of the Germans in the Ardennes and the victorious advance into Austria and Czechoslovakia, while quietly forgetting that Cobra succeeded because the British and Canadians held most of the German armour around Caen (the US Army didn't face a Tiger in Normandy), that the US Army had its fair selection of failure from Kasserine to the Schnee Eiffel and, of course, the shocking pursuit of glory rather than the enemy by Mark Clark in Italy.

The British and Commonwealth troops, with their old-fashioned helmets, spring-powered PIAT anti-tank weapons and veneration of heroic defeats, may have lost the propaganda war – in spite of its quality, the cut of a British Army battledress blouse probably did that on day 1 – but their record speaks for itself. They may have started badly in France and the Far East, but they were victorious in the North African desert against first the Italians and then the Germans. After this they took a major role in the invasions of Sicily and Italy and knocked the Italians out of the war, before invading and liberating north-west Europe. They held back the might of the Panzers in Normandy, chased the Germans back into the Netherlands and came within a whisker at Arnhem of circumventing the Siegfried Line – in spite of an airplan that seemed determined to make life harder for the paras than help them – and won battle after battle against a fanatic defence on their way to final victory. In Burma and India, after the initial attacks took the Japanese to the Indian borders, the Forgotten Army – created in 1943 – first held the Japanese and then inflicted at Imphal and Kohima the greatest loss to the Japanese on land, before rolling them back and retaking the territory lost in late 1941 and early 1942, reaching Rangoon just in time before the 1945 monsoon thanks to a brilliant all-arms campaign.

Then there are the British generals, universally classified as donkeys, particularly inspirational leader Bernard Montgomery. His abrasive style and – to his American allies at least – unintelligible English, added to his careful and methodical approach

to battle, infuriated the US press corps as well as a variety of detractors including British Air Marshal Tedder and American General George Patton – whose personal self-belief would only gain significant widespread traction for posterity after George C. Scott's brilliant portrayal on film in 1970. Tactically they may have been at sixes and sevens in 1940–41, but by 1942 they had the tactical nous, the battle-hardened units, the necessary weapons and capable commanders to take the fight to their enemies. British air–land cooperation in Africa formed the basis for future Allied tactical air operations; the commandos were the blueprint for postwar special forces; the Parachute Regiment an elite unit second to none; and British artillery was probably the best in the world in 1945, and if not, then certainly *primus inter pares*. As for the poor bloody infantryman, British footsloggers – and the other nationalities who served alongside them: Australians, New Zealanders, Belgians, Canadians, French, Indians, Poles, South Africans, etc – proved themselves as good as any opposition, if not as fanatical as the *Hitlerjugend* or other German units that had lost their moral compass helping out the *Einsatzgruppen* in Russia. Recent research by modern writers and academics – such as Stephen Badsley, John Buckley, Terry Copp and Stephen Hart – has done much to balance some of the lazy views expressed about the British infantryman. This book attempts to continue this theme.

ABOVE Men from the East Yorkshire Regiment Living History Group who gave generously of their time and knowledge to help supply photographs for this book. Back row, left to right: Dave Hebden, Adam Heaton, Andrew Dixon, Ed Hallett, Martin Clewlow, Karl Mason, Bill Pozniak. Front row: Dale Heaton, Gary Hancock, Tim Shellcock, Michael Lycett.

Chapter Two

Organisation

Britain's European defence policy was predicated on sending troops to help the French Army defend against any German attack through the Low Countries. The trouble was that this commitment came well down the list of defence spending priorities. However, for all the lack of preparedness, British Imperial forces had a basic strength: all had been organised, trained and equipped along the same pattern, which meant they meshed together and fought with few organisational or logistical difficulties.

OPPOSITE British troops arrive in France in 1939. By the end of September that year the BEF had 152,000 men in France. By the time the Germans attacked, this had increased to ten infantry divisions.

British forces worldwide in 1939

Britain stood alone in 1940, we are always told, but that's not the whole story. In 1939 British politics were the politics of empire and British forces were very much set up to provide a defence of its global territories. It is worth bearing this in mind when considering the defence spending of the 1920s and 1930s. The Secretary of State for War emphasised the order of importance in a December 1936 memorandum:

The Army has three main functions to perform. It has to maintain garrisons overseas in various parts of the Empire, to provide the military share in Home Defence, including Anti-Aircraft Defence, Coast Defence and Internal Security, and lastly, in time of emergency or war, to provide a properly equipped force ready to proceed overseas wherever it may be wanted.

Britain was increasingly prepared to fight in Europe but the costs would have to be shared with worldwide considerations: the *Annual Review of Imperial Defence Policy* for 1933 said 'expenditure of the Defence Departments should be governed by . . . the Defence of our possessions and interests in the Far East;

European Commitments; the Defence of India'. It went on to say: 'No expenditure should for the present be incurred on measures of defence required to provide exclusively against attack by the United States, France or Italy!'

Britain increasingly expected to have to fight in Europe, although to begin with felt that they should resist the need for the cost of a British expeditionary force. In February 1936 a Ministerial Sub-Committee on Defence Policy and Requirements recommended that 'the rate of mobilisation should be accelerated in order to make possible the disembarkation of [the Regular Field Force] on the Continent within a fortnight', but still the emphasis was on coastal defence and anti-aircraft defences.

Britain was allied with France – on paper, the strongest of the Western European powers with significant, modern armed forces: a standing army of 900,000 with some 5 million reservists, around 10,500 artillery pieces, over 4,000 tanks, nearly 3,000 aircraft and a substantial navy. With that and the Maginot Line protecting its eastern flank, France looked like a strong bulwark against potential German aggression, although, as we now know, this was far from the case: on 10 May 1940, when France's 1,130 battalions went to war, many of the men were tied down in fortresses and most of the Type A reserves had barely a year's training. Their tanks were better armoured than

saw the first action in which an Australian general led an Australian division in an attack planned by Australian staff. ❻

- **7th Division**: formed in 1940, it fought in the Middle East (Lebanon and Syria) during which two VCs were awarded, and over a thousand casualties sustained. In December 1941 the division was returned to Australia – rather than Burma as requested by the British government – and it next saw action in New Guinea and then Borneo. ❼
- **8th Division**: raised in July 1940, by the end of February 1942 the division's men had been defeated and entered captivity from Singapore, Rabaul, Ambon and Timor. The division lost 2,500 dead and 7,500 wounded and captured. The captured lost one in three in the awful privations of the Japanese prison camps.
- **9th Division**: the heroes of Tobruk, the division was formed in the UK in 1940 and sent to Cyrenaica in 1941. It fought through the North African campaign losing 5,800 casualties including 1,225 dead in the fighting at the First and Second Battles of El Alamein. In October 1942 the division returned to Australia, fighting in New Guinea and Borneo. In total, just over 12,000 casualties were sustained, including 2,732 killed in action. ❽
- **10th Division**: raised in April and disbanded in August 1942.
- **11th Division**: fought in New Guinea and New Britain.

Canada

Over a million Canadians served in the Canadian armed forces: 42,000 were killed and 55,000 wounded. The Canadian Army enlisted 730,000 and – of the half that went overseas – they served all over the globe, including Hong Kong (nearly 2,000 men in two battalions: 290 died in the fighting and nearly 270 in captivity) and the Aleutian Islands, although most of their efforts were in north-west Europe. In 1940, during and after the fighting in France, Canada provided materiel – over 50 million rounds of small-arms ammunition and 75,000 Ross rifles – as well as manpower, helping to defend the West Indies, and Iceland, after its occupation in June 1940. On 12 June 1940, the 1st Canadian

ABOVE In autumn 1943, the British Army was running short of junior officers. The Canloan scheme was devised to allow Canadian officers to volunteer to serve in the British Army. The memorial in Ottawa records that '673 Canadian Officers volunteered for loan to the British Army and took part in the invasion and liberation of Europe 1944–45. Canloan total casualties were 465, of which 128 were fatal'. These Canloan officers – Lt W.A. Harvie and Capt Philip H. Turner – served with the 2nd Battalion, South Staffordshire Regiment at Arnhem. *(Library and Archives Canada PA-169958)*

RIGHT 1st Canadian Parachute Battalion shoulder insignia. Assigned to British 6th Airborne Division, Canadian paras fought with great distinction in Normandy, dropping to destroy vital bridges on the east flank. The battalion also fought as ground troops during the Battle of the Bulge and dropped over the Rhine during Operation Varsity in 1945.

Infantry Brigade went to Brittany as a part of the second British Expeditionary Force but its stay was limited and it re-embarked on 18 June. Canadian troops then helped with British Home Defence – they were situated on the Channel coast and would have been in the front line if a German invasion had taken place. Meanwhile, Canada continued to supply food, weapons and materiel. Eight Canadian infantry divisions were raised:

- **1st Division** (formation patch red): fought in Sicily, Italy and after Operation Goldflake – when the Canadian forces were moved to north-west Europe – with First Canadian Army.
- **2nd Division** (blue): first saw action during the disastrous Operation Jubilee (Dieppe)

and, after reconstruction, with British Second Army during the invasion of Normandy. It went on to fight with First Canadian Army along the Channel coast, including the Scheldt clearance, before being part of the liberation of the Netherlands.

- **3rd Division** (light blue): assaulted on D-Day (Juno Beach) as part of British Second Army before passing over to First Canadian Army when it became operational, fighting along the Channel, clearing Breskens Pocket, and on into the Netherlands.
- **6th Division** (red and blue diagonal halves): raised in 1942, in 1943 a brigade went to the Aleutians but didn't see action; returned to Canada.
- **7th Division** (light blue and green diagonal halves): mobilised in 1942 and used for home defence.
- **8th Division** (green and brown diagonal halves): raised 1942, disbanded 1943.

India

British India declared war on Germany in September 1939. Over 2.5 million Indians fought for the British during the war – 40% of them muslims – and the country would win its independence as a result. Auchinleck, Commander-in-Chief of the Indian Army from 1942, said that Britain 'couldn't have come through both wars [World Wars I and II] if they hadn't had the Indian Army'. It's certainly true that India provided men – 87,000 of them died – money and materiel and without this the Japanese would certainly have not been stopped at Imphal and Kohima. The infantry divisions involved were:

- **3rd Division**: the Chindits – their military importance may be debatable but their bravery never can be doubted.
- **4th Division**: fought in East Africa, North Africa and Italy, ending up in Greece. Some 6 British and 15 Indian battalions; over 25,000 casualties, 4 VCs.
- **5th Division:** fought in East Africa, North Africa, at Kohima and Imphal and then Burma – the first unit into Singapore in 1945. The main elements were 6 British and 17 Indian battalions.
- **6th Division**: created in 1941, fought in Iraq

Monty felt that:

Regimental spirit and tradition can be a powerful factor in making for good morale, and must be constantly encouraged. But in the crisis of battle a man will not derive encouragement from the glories of the past; he will seek aid from his leaders and comrades of the present. Most men do not fight well because their ancestors fought well at the Battle of Minden two centuries ago, but because their particular platoon or unit has good leaders, is well disciplined, and has developed the feelings of comradeship and self-respect among all ranks and on all levels. It is not devotion to some ancient regimental story that steels men in the crisis; it is devotion to the comrades who are with them and the leaders who are in front of them.

Originally, most regiments had only one battalion, but the expansion of the empire saw two battalions become the norm; one overseas, the other in Britain where it could act as a recruiting and training centre. All this changed when warfare went global and regiments had to increase in size to accommodate the huge extra manpower required – the First World War regiments were often ten or more battalions strong. However, the 1918 armistice saw the start of a major contraction – although there were still many overseas requirements for extra men: garrisons in Germany, the fighting in Ireland (the Free State was finally established in 1922), assistance for the White Russians against the Bolsheviks (1918–20) and the Third Afghan War of 1919 all helped put off some of the inevitable changes to the peacetime army.

Nevertheless, the 1920s saw alterations and reductions. Most regiments were cut back to two battalions and the reorganisation of the cavalry in 1921–22 saw amalgamations. Also in 1922, after the creation of the Irish Free State, the southern Irish regiments were disbanded: Connaught Rangers, Prince of Wales's Leinster Regiment (Royal Canadians), Royal Dublin Fusiliers, Royal Irish Regiment and Royal Munster Fusiliers. The increase in size of the army as war approached saw

the pendulum swing once more. The ranks were swelled and new battalions had to be formed. The British Army started the Second World War with 69 infantry regiments: 5 in the Brigade of Guards and 64 infantry of the line. This number was increased during the war by the formation of the Parachute and Glider Pilot Regiments (both part of the Army Air Corps) in 1942 and the Special Air Service joined the AAC in 1944. The infantry regiments in 1939 are listed below in their order of precedence, along with the abbreviations identified in the *Field Service Pocket Book*:

Brigade of guards
Grenadier Guards (Gren Gds)
Coldstream Guards (Coldm Gds)
Scots Guards (SG)
Irish Guards (IG)
Welsh Guards (WG)

Infantry of the line

The 64 foot regiments were numbered, as the US *Handbook of the British Army* enumerates, between 1 and 91, the missing numbers being disbanded regiments, or allotted to junior battalions of existing regiments. No 18, for example, belonged to the Royal Irish Regiment mentioned above, which was disbanded in 1922. No 52 was the 2nd Battalion of the 43rd Regiment, all of whose battalions are known as the Oxfordshire and Buckinghamshire Light Infantry.

BELOW Metal titles could be worn on the shoulder straps of service dress tunics, khaki drill jackets and greatcoat. This one is for the East Surrey Regiment.

Typical shoulder and arm cloth badges, from top to bottom: East Yorkshire shoulder flash; 3rd Infantry Division insignia; red arm of service line identifying infantry; a Yorkshire rose on a black background – a special identification for the 2nd East Yorks, the black remembering General Wolfe who fell in victory at Quebec. Finally, the crown and chevrons of a colour sergeant (in this case) or CQMS. The shoulder flashes changed during the war. In ACI 905, dated 12 June 1943, the colour of the background and the lettering were mandated as was the text of the regimental designation. The infantry was set as scarlet with white lettering (as here). For a full list of infantry regiment designations see the table on pages 32–33.

BRITISH REGIMENTS OF FOOT

No	Regiment	Official abbreviation	1943 shoulder flash designation, if different
1	The Royal Scots (The Royal Regiment)	RS	Royal Scots
2	The Queen's Royal Regiment (West Surrey)	Queen's	
3	The Buffs (Royal East Kent Regiment)	Buffs	
4	The King's Own Royal Regiment (Lancaster)	King's Own	
5	The Royal Northumberland Fusiliers	NF	R Northumberland Fus
6	The Royal Warwickshire Regiment	Warwick	Royal Warwickshire
7	The Royal Fusiliers (City of London Regiment)	RF	Royal Fusiliers
8	The King's Regiment (Liverpool)	King's	The King's Regiment
9	The Royal Norfolk Regiment	Norfolk	Royal Norfolk
10	The Lincolnshire Regiment	Lincolns	Lincoln
11	The Devonshire Regiment	Devon	
12	The Suffolk Regiment	Suffolk	
13	The Somerset Light Infantry (Prince Albert's)	Som LI	Somerset LI
14	The West Yorkshire Regiment (The Prince of Wales's Own)	WYorks	West Yorkshire
15	The East Yorkshire Regiment (The Duke of York's Own)	EYorks	East Yorkshire
16	The Bedfordshire and Hertfordshire Regiment	Bedfs Herts	Bedfs and Herts
17	The Leicestershire Regiment	Leicesters	Leicestershire
19	The Green Howards (Alexandra, Princess of Wales's Own Yorkshire Regiment)	Green Howards	
20	The Lancashire Fusiliers	LF	Lancashire Fusiliers
21	The Royal Scots Fusiliers	RSF	Royal Scots Fusiliers
22	The Cheshire Regiment	Cheshire	
23	The Royal Welch Fusiliers	RWF	Royal Welch Fusiliers
24	The South Wales Borderers	SWB	
25	The King's Own Scottish Borderers	KOSB	
26	The Cameronians (Scottish Rifles)	Cameronians	
27	The Royal Inniskilling Fusiliers	Innisks	Inniskillings
28	The Gloucestershire Regiment	Glosters	Gloster
29	The Worcestershire Regiment	WorcR	Worcestershire
30	The East Lancashire Regiment	ELanR	East Lancashire
31	The East Surrey Regiment	Surreys	East Surrey
32	The Duke of Cornwall's Light Infantry	DCLI	Cornwall
33	The Duke of Wellington's Regiment (West Riding)	DWR	Duke of Wellington's
34	The Border Regiment	Border	
35	The Royal Sussex Regiment	RSussex	Royal Sussex
37	The Hampshire Regiment	Hamps	Hampshire
38	The South Staffordshire Regiment	SStaffords	South Stafford
39	The Dorsetshire Regiment	Dorset	
40	The South Lancashire Regiment (The Prince of Wales's Volunteer)	PWV	South Lancashire
41	The Welch Regiment	Welch	Welch Regiment
42	The Black Watch (Royal Highland Regiment)	Black Watch	a tartan patch
43	The Oxfordshire and Buckinghamshire Light Infantry	OxfBucks	Oxf & Bucks
44	The Essex Regiment	Essex	
45	The Sherwood Foresters (Nottinghamshire and Derbyshire Regiment)	Foresters	
47	The Loyal Regiment (North Lancashire)	Loyals	
48	The Northamptonshire Regiment	Northamptons	Northamptonshire
49	The Royal Berkshire Regiment (Princess Charlotte of Wales's)	RBerks	Royal Berkshire
50	The Queen's Own Royal West Kent Regiment	RWK	Royal West Kent
51	The King's Own Yorkshire Light Infantry	KOYLI	
53	The King's Shropshire Light Infantry	KSLI	

No	Regiment	Official abbreviation	1943 shoulder flash designation, if different
57	The Middlesex Regiment (Duke of Cambridge's Own)	Mx	Middlesex
60	The King's Royal Rifle Corps	KRRC	
62	The Wiltshire Regiment (Duke of Edinburgh's)	Wilts	Wiltshire
63	The Manchester Regiment	Manch	Manchester
64	The North Staffordshire Regiment (The Prince of Wales's)	NStaffs	North Staffords
65	The York and Lancaster Regiment	Y&L	York and Lancaster
68	The Durham Light Infantry	DLI	Durham LI
71	The Highland Light Infantry (City of Glasgow Regiment)	HLI	a tartan patch
72	The Seaforth Highlanders (Ross-shire Buffs, the Duke of Albany's)	Seaforth	a tartan patch
75	The Gordon Highlanders	Gordons	a tartan patch
79	The Queen's Own Cameron Highlanders	Camerons	a tartan patch
83	The Royal Ulster Rifles	RUR	Royal Ulster Rifles
87	The Royal Irish Fusiliers (Princess Victoria's)	RIrF	Royal Irish Fusiliers
91	The Argyll and Sutherland Highlanders (Princess Louise's)	A&SH	A and SH
None	The Rifle Brigade (Prince Consort's Own)	RB	Rifle Brigade

Infantry battalion	Regt RAC
5/King's Own	107th
1/5 LF	108th
1/6 LF	109th
5/Border	110th
5/Manch	111th
9/Foresters	112th
2/5 WYorks	113th
2/6 DWR	114th
2/7 DWR	115th
9/Gordons	116th
7/Buffs	141st
7/Suffolk	142nd
9/LF	143rd
8/ELanR	144th
8/DWR	145th
9/DWR	146th
10/Hamps	147th
9/Loyals	148th
7/KOYLI	149th
10/Y&L	150th
10/King's Own	151st
11/King's	152nd
8/Essex	153rd
9/NStaffs	154th
15/DLI	155th
11/HLI	156th
9/Hamps	157th
9/SWB	158th
10/Glosters	159th
9/RSussex	160th
12/Green Howards	161st
9/RWK	162nd
13/Foresters	163rd

A number of infantry battalions were converted to RAC Regiments in 1941 and 1942 as the expansion of armoured units became necessary. This is shown in the table, left.

These regiments did not fight as one unit but contributed battalions to larger formations as required. This meant that regiments could be spread around the globe. An example of this is shown in the history of the East Yorkshire Regiment (for more details see pages 72–76): 1st Battalion served in India (1939–42) and then Burma; 2nd Battalion fought in France with the BEF and then assaulted on D-Day; 4th Battalion fought in France in 1940 and then the North African desert; 5th Battalion fought in Africa and Sicily before it, too, assaulted on D-Day; 6th Battalion was a Home Guard battalion; 7th Battalion was disbanded in July 1944, its men serving as replacements; and 8th was raised as an AA battalion.

Most British infantry battalions were rifle battalions; some were motorised – some lorried but others, usually those in armoured divisions (often KRRC and RB units), in Bren carriers or, latterly, US halftracks. The MG battalions and Reconnaissance troops (initially a Divisional Recce Regt, after 1941 units from the newly formed Reconnaissance Corps) were also motorised.

In major unit terms, therefore, the battalion was the building block of British infantry forces (see the table Organisation of an

TABLE 1
ORGANISATION OF AN INFANTRY BATTALION April 1943–45

Battalion HQ (5 Offr 45 ORs)
CO is a Lt Col; 2IC (a Major); Adjutant (Capt/Lt); RSM (WOI); Intelligence section (1 offr 7 ORs); RAP (attached RAMC MO with 22 men, Chaplain and driver); Police (4 men); from 1944 Sniper section (8 men) – before these were in Coy HQs. On the move little distinction between Bn HQ and HQ Coy. There was usually a forward HQ (tactical, run by the CO with adjutant, signals and intelligence officers) and a rear (run by 2IC, with transport, supply and maintenance elements).

HQ Company (Coy HQ, 1 Offr 5 ORs, plus Nos 1–2 Pl = 3 Offr 86 ORs; Total 4 Offr 91 ORs)

- **1 Platoon** (Signals) 1 Offr, 35 ORs
  Controlled communications between Bn and Bde HQ and Bn subunits – telephones (2 10-line switchboards, 8 D or L telephone sets – increased to 14 for the battalion by July 1944– 6 H telephone sets for three Observation posts), 6 Fuller phones, 14–15 miles of cable (either D3 or PVC assault cable), DRs, and radios – No 18 set used by RSigs personnel for Bn net; 4 installed in carriers. From 1942 No 38 sets issued to and used by infantrymen – 7 to Mortar Pl for each carrier; 6 to the Carrier Pl; 2 to each Rifle Coy (1 to HQ, 1 to one of the Rifle Pl).

- **2 Platoon** (Admin) 2 Offr, 51 ORs
  12 3-ton lorries (5 rations and cook; 1 Officers mess and HQ Coy cooks; 1 with 2in mortar rounds; 1 with 3in mortar rounds; 1 petrol; 1 QM stores; 1 MT stores; 1 rations (towed 180gal water trailer); various mechanics/clerks/etc

Support Company (Coy HQ, 1 Offr 8 ORs, plus Nos 3–6 Pl = 7 Offr 184 ORs; Total 7 Offr 190 ORs)
Before 1943 HQ company had these platoons.

- **3 Platoon** (Mortar) 1 Offr 43 ORs
  OC Capt; equipment included a carrier; From 1944 HQ and 3 sections (each 2 detachments each with a 3in mortar). By 1944 HQ carrier had an 18 and 38 set; the carriers all had 38s and six further spare 38s were carried.

- **4 Platoon** (Carrier) 2 Offr 58 ORs
  OC Capt; PL HQ carrier plus 2 15cwt trucks and 3 motorcycles
  Each section Carrier 1 – Sgt, Bren gunners 1 and 2, driver/mechanic; Bren gun, PIAT. Carriers 2/3 – Cpl, Bren gunners 1 and 2, driver/mechanic; Bren gun plus 2in mortar in one carrier. Used to support rifle sections. Wasp flame-thrower carriers allocated 8 per battalion held by Ordnance depots until required.

- **5 Platoon** (Anti-tank) 2 Offr 56 ORs
  OC Capt, 2IC subaltern; 3 sections each 2 guns (2pdrs, replaced by 6pdrs) towed by Loyd carriers. No wireless comms

- **6 Platoon** (Assault pioneer) 1 Offr 25 ORs
  OC Capt; tradesmen (carpenters, bricklayer, mason) 10 Pioneers. From 1943 Pioneer section (tradesmen) in 3-ton lorry; 2 Assault Sects (each 4 pioneers under command of a Cpl) used for mine removal (mine detector sets) and obstacle destruction (Bangalore torpedoes, Lifebuoy flamethrowers; No 75 grenades.

A Company (Nos 7–9 Pl) 5 Offr 122 ORs

- **Company HQ** (2 offr 12 ORs – 14 in 1943 with snipers)
  OC Major; 2IC Capt; CSM, CQMS, Coy clerk, 9 ORs (drivers, orderlies, batmen; 2 x snipers were moved to Bn HQ in November 1944). Carrier allocated from 1943.

- **7 Platoon** (1 offr 36 ORs)
  - **Platoon HQ** (7 men)
    OC Lt or 2-Lt (one of the three platoons; other two command by WOIII; 2IC Sgt (for a while the WOIII PISM); 2 ORs (signaller/batman, Orderly/Runner); Mortar Det (LCpl commander with 2 ORs)
  - **Section** (10 ORs)
    Rifle group (Sect commander (Cpl); 6 x riflemen); Gun group (Section 2IC (LCpl); 2 ORs)
  - **Section** (10 ORs)
  - **Section** (10 ORs)
- **8 Platoon** (1 offr 36 ORs)
- **9 Platoon** (1 offr 36 ORs)
- **B Company** (Nos 10–12 Pl)
- **C Company** (Nos 13–15 Pl)
- **D Company** (Nos 16–18 Pl)

Total personnel		Total vehicles		Total weapons	
Officers	33–36	Bikes	33	Rifles	583
WOs	7–8	Motorbikes	26	SMGs	178
SSgts	5–6	Trucks 15cwt	30	LMGs	63
Sgts	34–38	Lorries 3-ton	14	PIAT	23
Cpl	71–72	Loyd carriers	12	2in mortars	26
Pvt	656–685	Universal carriers	19	3in mortars	6
Total	806–845	Universal carriers (mor)	7	Signal pistols	39

TABLE 2
ORGANISATION OF AN INFANTRY DIVISION 1944

- **Div HQ**
- **3 x Infantry Brigades** each with HQ and 3 x Inf Bns (see Table 1)
- **Reconnaissance Regiment** each with HQ Sqn (inc Support Group of Sig Tp, Mor Tp, ATk Bty, Admin Tp) and 3 x Recce Sqns (each with Sqn HQ, 3 x Recce Tp – each with 2 armoured cars, 3 light reconnaissance cars and 6 carriers – and an Assault Tp with Tp HQ and 4 sects of 8 ORs)
- **Division RA** (HQ, 3 x Fd Arty Regts, 1 x ATk Regt and 1 x LAA Regt)
- **Division RE** (HQ, 3 x Fd Coys, 1 x Fd Park Coy, 1 x Div Bridging Pl)
- **Division Signals**
- **MG Battalion** (HQ Coy, Heavy Mortar Coy with 4 x Platoons of 4 x 4.2in mortars, 3 x MG Coys with 3 x Platoons each of 4 MMGs)

Total vehicles		Total weapons	
Carriers	595	Rifles	12,265
Armoured cars	63	SMGs	6,525
Trucks and Lorries	1,937	LMGs	1,262
		MMGs	40
Total personnel		2in/3in/4.2in mortars	359
		PIATs	436
Officers	870	25pdrs	72
ORs	17,477	ATk guns (6pdr/17pdr)	110
Total	18,347	AA guns (20mm/40mm)	125

- **Division Ordnance** (Ord Field Park, MLBU)
- **Div Postal Unit**
- **Div Provost Coy**
- **Division REME** (3 x Inf Bde workshops)
- **Medical** (inc 3 x Fd Amb sects, 2 x Fd Dressing Stations)
- **Division RASC**

---

infantry battalion on the left). Commanded by a lieutenant colonel, most battalions were grouped with others to form a brigade, commanded by a brigadier. There were usually three battalions in a brigade and three brigades formed a division. Brigades could be independent and comprise all-arms units – including armour, artillery etc – but usually they were part of a division (see the table Organisation of an infantry division on the left). In total over 175 British infantry brigades were formed during the war – some of them started off as AA brigades, a number were deception units and some didn't exist for very long.

Divisions

The arm of a British division was identified by its title – airborne, anti-aircraft, armoured or infantry – but armoured divisions contained infantry and infantry divisions had attached armour. Increasingly as the war progressed and all-arms tactics were developed, formations were made up of a combination of all-arms units with direct links to the main bulk of the artillery – in north-west Europe grouped together by army – and air support.

There were 40 infantry divisions in the British Army during the Second World War: a mixture of Regular Army and Territorial. The Territorial divisions were divided into first- and second-line formations. The Secretary of State for War made an announcement on 29 March 1939 that the Territorial Army was to be increased in numbers from 130,000 to 170,000, and subsequently doubled to 340,000. This massive increase would

TERRITORIAL ARMY INFANTRY DIVISIONS	
First line	**Second line**
1st London (Later 56th (London))	2nd London (Later 47th (London))
42nd (East Lancashire)	66th
43rd (Wessex)	45th
44th (Home Counties)	12th (Eastern)
48th (South Midland)	61st
49th (West Riding)	46th
50th (Northumbrian)	23rd (Northumbrian)
51st (Highland)	9th (Highland)
52nd (Lowland)	15th (Scottish)
53rd (Welsh)	38th (Welsh)
54th (East Anglian)	18th
55th (West Lancashire)	59th (Staffordshire)

require each of the current first-line TA units to form duplicate, second-line versions. For example (see table opposite), 1st London Division's second-line duplicate was 2nd London Division.

The relationship between the Regulars and the Territorials was complex; both had proved averse to the progressive reforms that the General Staff proposed in the interwar period. The TA was always an important part of defence policy both at home and abroad. The Regular Army was too small to be able to deal with any large-scale conflict without reinforcement: the TA supplied the reserve necessary to do so. In particular, especially after the effectiveness of air warfare was shown during the Spanish Civil War, the TA's anti-aircraft artillery role became increasingly important in the 1930s.

ABOVE Lt Gen Władysław Anders, commander of Polish II Corps, confers with Lt Gen Charles Keightley, GOC British 78th Division, at his HQ at Cervaro near Monte Cassino, 5 April 1944. Note the 78th Division Battleaxe patch, the Welsh Guards shoulder insignia and Keightley's general's collar gorget patches.

LEFT The 49th (West Riding) Infantry Division took part in the ill-fated Norwegian campaign before garrisoning Iceland 1941–42 – accounting for the Polar Bear divisional insignia. The photograph was taken on 2 May 1945 in Wageningen while the Polar Bears were part of the First Canadian Army. (*Nationaalarchief.nl*)

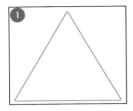

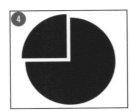

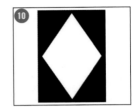

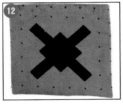

ABOVE The Pegasus insignia was used for both Airborne Divisions (1st and 6th) – see pp. 40–41. *(1, 4–6, 8, 10, 13 svg/WikiCommons; 9 EF; 2, 3, 7, 11, 12 RPJ Militaria)*

The British wartime infantry divisions were:

- **1st Division**: France September 1939–June 1940, North Africa March–December 1943, Italy December 1943–January 1945, then Palestine.
- **1st London Division**: TA. Redesignated 56th (London) Division 18 November 1940.
- **2nd Division**: France September 1939–May 1940, India June 1942–April 1944, Burma April 1944–April 1945, then India. ②
- **2nd London Division**: TA. Reformed 1939. Renamed 47th (London) Division on 18 November 1940; redesignated 47th Infantry (Reserve) Division on 1 September 1944.
- **3rd Division**: France and Belgium September 1939–June 1940, north-west Europe June 1944 on. ③
- **4th Division**: France and Belgium September 1939–June 1940, North Africa March–December 1943, Egypt December 1943–February 1944, Italy February–December 1944, and Greece December 1944 on. ④
- **5th Division**: France September 1939–June 1940, India May–August 1942, Iraq August–September 1942, Persia September 1942–January 1943, Syria February–June 1943, Egypt June 1943, Sicily July–September 1943, Italy September 1943–July 1944, Palestine July 1944–February 1945, and north-west Europe from March 1945 on. ⑤
- **6th Division**: Formed on 3 November 1939, by renaming of 7th Division. Dissolved June 1940 to become HQ Western Desert Force. Reformed on 17 February 1941. Renamed 70th Division

on 10 October 1941. ⑥ In 1943 6th Airborne Division created. ⑦

- **7th Division**: Based in Palestine 1939. Moved to Egypt and on 3 November 1939 redesignated 6th Division.
- **8th Division**: Based in Palestine in 1939. Disbanded 28 February 1940. ⑧
- **9th (Highland) Division:** TA. Formed September 1939. On 7 August 1940 redesignated 51st (Highland) Division. ⑨
- **12th (Eastern) Division**: TA. Formed 10 October 1939. Served in France April–June 1940. Disbanded 11 July 1940. ⑩
- **12th Division**: Formed 11 July 1942 in the Sudan, from 1st Sudan Defence Force Brigade. On 12 January 1945 redesignated Sudan Defence Force Group (North Africa).
- **15th (Scottish) Division**: TA. Formed September 1939. North-west Europe from 14 June 1944 on. ⑪
- **18th Division**: TA. Formed 30 September 1939. India January 1942, Malaya (incl. Singapore) February 1942. On 15 February 1942 captured by Imperial Japanese Army in Malaya. Fought on Singapore Island. ⑫
- **23rd (Northumbrian) Division**: TA. Formed 2 October 1939. France April–June 1940. Disbanded 30 June 1940. ⑬
- **36th Division**: Formed 1 September 1944 in Burma by redesignation of 36th Indian Infantry Division. Burma September 1944–May 1945, India May 1945 on.
- **38th (Welsh) Division**: TA. Activated on 18 September 1939. UK home defence; Lower Establishment on 1 December 1941. Disbanded 15 August 1944. Reformed

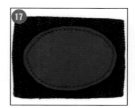
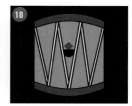
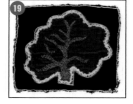

1 September 1944 as the 38th Infantry (Reserve) Division, Western Command's training formation.

■ **42nd (East Lancs) Division**: TA. Belgium and France April–June 1940. Redesignated 42nd Armoured Division on 1 November 1941.

■ **43rd (Wessex) Division**: TA. North-west Europe from 24 June 1944 on.

■ **44th (Home Counties) Division**: TA. France and Belgium April–June 1940, Egypt July 1942–January 1943. Disbanded 31 December 1943.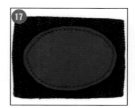

■ **45th Division:** TA. Formed September 1939. Dispersed August 1944. Redesignated 45th (Holding) Division 1 September 1944 and redesignated 45th Division 1 December 1944.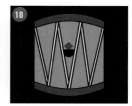

■ **46th Division**: TA. Formed 2 October 1939 in the UK. France and Belgium April–June 1940, North Africa January–September 1943, Italy September 1943–March 1944, Egypt in March 1944, Palestine April–June 1944, Egypt June 1944, Italy July 1944–January 1945, Greece January–April 1945, Italy April–May 1945, Austria as an occupation force.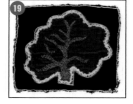

■ **47th (London) Division**: TA. Formed 21 November 1940 in the UK by redesignation of the 2nd London Division. Dispersed August 1944. Redesignated 47th Infantry (Reserve) Division 1 September 1944.

■ **48th (South Midland) Division**: TA. France and Belgium January–June 1940. Redesignated 48th Infantry (Reserve) Division 20 December 1942.

■ **49th (West Riding) Division**: TA. Disbanded 5 April 1940 and reconstituted 10 June 1940. North-west Europe 12 June 1944 on.

■ **50th (Northumbrian) Division**: TA. France and Belgium January–June 1940, Egypt June–July 1941, Cyprus July–November 1941, Syria January–February 1942, Egypt February 1942, Libya February–June 1942, Egypt June–December 1942, Libya December 1942–March 1943, North Africa March–April 1943, Libya April–May 1943, Egypt May–June 1943, Sicily July–October 1943, north-west Europe June–December 1944. Redesignated an Infantry (Reserve) Division in the UK 16 December 1944. Norway August 1945 as HQ British Land Forces Norway.

■ **51st (Highland) Division**: TA. France 24 January–June 1940. Captured at Saint-Valery-en-Caux 12 June 1940. Reconstituted as 9th (Highland) Infantry Division 7 August 1940, Egypt August–November 1942, Libya November 1942–February 1943, North Africa February–July 1943, north-west Europe from June 1944 on.

■ **52nd (Lowland) Division**: TA. Trained as a mountain and airlanding division, but never used in either role. France June 1940, north-west Europe October 1944 on.

■ **53rd (Welsh) Division**: TA. North-west Europe June 1944 on.

■ **54th (East Anglian) Division**: TA. Disbanded in the United Kingdom 14 December 1943.

(14–17, 19–27 RPJ Militaria; 18, svg/ WikiCommons) WikiCommons)

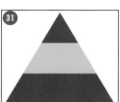

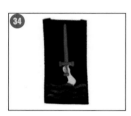

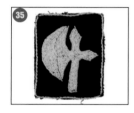

(28–30, 32–35 RPJ Militaria; 31, 36, svg/ WikiCommons)

■ **55th (West Lancashire) Division**: TA. Ended the war under Western Command. ㉘

■ **56th (London) Division**: Formed 18 November 1940 by redesignation of the 1st London Division. Iraq November 1942–March 1943, Palestine March 1943, Egypt March–April 1943, Libya April 1943, Libya May–August 1943, Italy September 1943–March 1944, Egypt April–July 1944, Italy July 1944 on. ㉙

■ **59th (Staffordshire) Division**: TA. Formed 4 September 1939 in the UK. North-west Europe June–October 1944. Disbanded 19 October 1944. ㉚

■ **61st Division**: TA. Division did not leave the UK. Northern Ireland 20 June 1940–February 1943. Reorganised August 1945 as a Light Division to deploy to fight Japan but war ended first.

■ **66th Division**: TA. Activated 27 September 1939. Broken up 23 June 1940 and dispersed to 1st London, 55th (West Lancashire) and 59th (Staffordshire) Divisions. ㉛

■ **70th Division**: Formed 10 October 1941, when the 6th Division replaced the Australian garrison in Tobruk. India on 10 March 1942. Broken up on 25 October 1943. ㉜

■ **76th Division**: Formed 18 November 1941 from Norfolk County Division. On 20 December 1942 the division was renamed the 76th Infantry (Reserve) Division and became Eastern Command's training formation. Disbanded 1 September 1944, and the 47th Infantry (Reserve) Division took its place. ㉝

■ **77th Division**: Formed 1 December 1941 from Devon and Cornwall County Division. On 20 December 1942 reorganised as the 77th Infantry (Reserve) Division, and became Northern Command's training formation. On 1 December 1943 reorganised to become the 77th Holding Division. Disbanded 1 September 1944. ㉞

■ **78th Division**: Formed 25 May 1942. North Africa November 1942–July 1943, Sicily July–September 1943, Italy September 1943–July 1944, Egypt July–September 1944, Italy September 1944–May 1945. Ended the war in Austria. ㉟

■ **80th (Reserve) Division**: Formed 1 January 1943 as Western Command's training formation. Disbanded 1 September 1944. ㊱

The infantry division establishments changed during wartime: in 1939, there were 13,863 men in total, three brigades each of three battalions, an MG battalion and three regiments of artillery for close support. By 1944 the establishment had grown to 18,347 (870 officers and 17,477 ORs) and included reconnaissance, LAA and anti-tank units. The normal grouping for mobile operations saw each of the brigade groups organised as follows:

■ Bde HQ, 3 × Inf Bns, MG Coy, Heavy mortar Platoon, Field Regiment (Artillery), Anti-tank Battery, Field Company, RASC, Field Ambulance, LAA Troop.

Infantry in armoured divisions

As well as infantry divisions, British armoured divisions included infantry units: usually motor battalions, sometimes lorried. The lorried infantry were organised like normal infantry but instead of marching they had motor transport. Motor battalions were organised differently, and latterly, equipped with US halftracks, gained more all-terrain mobility. The motor company included a carrier-borne recce platoon. The motor battalions were there to clear anti-tank obstacles the tanks couldn't deal with, then mop up after the armour. Lorried infantry were expected to do the same and also relieve motor battalion troops so they could get back to the tanks. They were also there to protect the armoured division while it was camped. However, until later in the war most of this fighting was unintegrated and saw few joint actions: the fighting was either a task for the tanks or the infantry.

The British concept of armoured units, developed in the interwar period, saw two types of tank and two types of unit: infantry and cruiser. The former – *Tank* brigades – supported the infantry; the latter – *Armoured* brigades – were designed for mobile warfare. This was the key point of the doctrine: cruiser tanks were designed for exploitation of success and pursuit, not fighting with the infantry. To promote this, there were two different types of tank (the *infantry* exemplified by the well-armoured but slow and undergunned Churchill that couldn't keep up if the battle became mobile) and the *cruiser* tanks which were faster, less well armoured and, unfortunately until later in the war, undergunned too: but that's another story. Both types of unit trained in different ways. Montgomery disliked the approach, preferring what he called the 'capital' tank (we'd call it universal today) best exemplified in his eyes by the Sherman.

The integration of armour and infantry in an armoured division was only really achieved in the later north-west European campaigns. Before then, the armoured division infantry establishments were there to allow the division to launch infantry attacks but there was not much integration: that took place between the infantry and the independent tank brigades, although there was little linked training. The mixed divisions saw improved cooperation between the two components, but they didn't last long and it would take bitter experiences in the early war years before proper infantry tank cooperation was achieved. The infantry component of the armoured divisions altered during the war. Timothy Harrison Place outlines it succinctly: 'Armour steadily lost its predominance as the war proceeded, the unit ratio of armour to infantry to artillery shifting from 6:2:2 in 1939 to 4:4:4 in 1945. May 1942 saw the armoured division lose an armoured brigade, gain an infantry brigade and double its artillery component.'

- In May 1939 the armoured division's support group included two motor battalions. This continued through the fighting in France.
- In October 1940 the armoured division's two armoured brigades were each given a motor battalion; the support group had a lorried infantry battalion.
- In May 1942, one of the two tank brigades was replaced by an infantry brigade of three lorried infantry battalions. The tank brigade retained its motor battalion.
- In the April 1943 establishment, and for the rest of the war, the armoured brigade included a motor battalion alongside a three-battalion infantry brigade. By 1944 the division also had an independent MG company.

There were three other types of motorised division with infantry components:

- 1st Cavalry Division: as a throwback to earlier times, on 31 October 1939 this division was re-formed. It would become 10th Armoured Division on 1 August 1941. It had three cavalry brigades each of which included two motorised infantry battalions.
- Three (of an intended six) TA divisions were created as motor divisions: 1st London, 50th (Northumbrian) and 55th (West Lancashire). These had two infantry brigades (each of three battalions and two anti-tank companies), an RA component of two artillery regiments and an anti-tank regiment and a total establishment of 10,136. The experiment didn't work and all became infantry divisions. Vehicles included:

Bicycles	220
Motorcycles	531
Combinations	99
Cars	103
Carriers	86
Ambulances	16
8cwt trucks	657
12cwt vans	17
Lorries	489
Fd artillery tractors	108

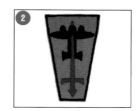
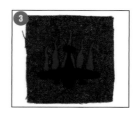

A selection of cloth badges – 1 The Netherlands badge was worn by the Prinses Irene Brigade; 2 the 1st AA and 3 the 5th AA Divisions; 4 the 218th Independent Infantry Brigade; 5 the Combined Operations badge worn by the Commandos.
(All: RPJ Militaria)

RIGHT Maj Gen Frederick 'Boy' Browning, husband of author Daphne Du Maurier, commanded 1st Airborne Division and 1 Airborne Corps during Operation Market Garden. He wears the shoulder strap of his regiment, the Grenadier Guards, and the Pegasus and Airborne insignia.

■ Between May 1942 and January 1943 seven infantry divisions became mixed divisions. The division concept didn't last long. Indeed, only one (4th Division) of the seven (1st, 3rd, 4th, 15th (Scottish), 43rd (Wessex), 53rd (Welsh) and 77th) saw action in this guise (in Tunisia). The mixed divisions were set up with two infantry

brigades and a tank brigade – in the case of the 4th Division, 21st Army Tank Brigade made up of 12th and 48th RTR and 145th RAC Regt. Its battles in Tunisia didn't go well (48RTR lost 38 Churchills in the battle for Tunis) and Monty didn't like the concept.

Other infantry divisions

From December 1942 reserve divisions were set up to hold personnel before sending them to their units. This allowed the other field army units to concentrate on their own training. There were four reserve divisions: 48th and 77th in Northern, 76th in Eastern and 80th in Western commands. In 1943 77th Division changed role, working with homecoming PoWs and those who had returned after service. September 1944 saw more changes. The 38th Infantry (Reserve) took over from 80th; 47th Infantry (Reserve) took over from 78th; 48th Infantry (Reserve) and 45th Infantry Holding took over from 77th.

Finally, to these should be added the Para divisions that were formed after the German Fallschirmjäger had impressed the Allies in the battle for Crete (ironically, at the same time, the Germans thought their losses made parachute operations unsustainable). Army Order 128 of 1 August created the Parachute Regiment with the motto *Utrinque Paratus* (Ready for anything!). The regiment raised 17 battalions during the war, creating two divisions (1st and 6th) who were either dropped or landed by glider in many wartime operations from clandestine insertions into France (such as the Bruneval Raid, Operation Biting, on 27–28 February 1942) to the major divisional landings in Normandy, Arnhem and over the Rhine. The Parachute Regiment became recognised for being elite soldiers – but the disaster at Arnhem showed the vulnerability of parachute infantry, however brave, without heavier supporting weapons. By August 1944 there were just over 12,000 men in an airborne division, some of whom were dropped by parachute, others by glider. Some made their way to the landing area by land (or sea in the case of D-Day). An airborne division would have comprised the following:

BELOW The armed forces of many European countries fought alongside the British Army. The Royal Netherlands Motorised Infantry Brigade – better known as the Prinses Irene Brigade (PIB) – landed in Normandy on 6 August and fought to the end of the war under British and Canadian command. Here a PIB 3in mortar crew prepare their bombs. Their insignia is a PIB shoulder flash and the lion and Nederland patch. (Nationaalarchief.nl)

- HQ
- Pathfinders, who were dropped first to identify the landing areas
- Paratroops, two brigades each of an HQ and Defence Pl, and three battalions (each HQ Coy and three Rifle Coys)
- Armoured Recce Regt, glider-borne, with HQ and HQ Sqn, Support Sqn and two Recce Sqns
- Airlanding Brigade, glider-borne, with HQ and Defence Pl, three battalions (each of six companies including four Rifle Coys of four platoons)
- Artillery including airborne FOU, Airlanding Light Regt (three batteries each of 8 × 75mm howitzers) and Airlanding ATk Regt (three batteries each of 6 × 6 or 17pdrs)
- Div troops – medical, RASC, RAOC, REME, etc
- Glider Pilot Regt personnel.

While discussing paratroops it's worth remembering that other nations were involved with the British forces. One of the para battalions that took part in the D-Day drop was 1st Canadian Para Battalion, assigned to 6th Airborne Division. It also took part in Operation Varsity and advanced to Wismar on the Baltic where it met Red Army troops. At Arnhem the Polish 1st Ind Parachute Brigade supported British paras at Oosterbeck. And, finally, the Indian Army had paras who had trained with the British. The 20th Indian Paratroop Brigade comprised 152nd Indian Para and 153rd Gurkha Para battalions and was under command of IV Corps. They took part in the capture of Rangoon, and on 1 May 1945 two battalions of Gurkha paratroops were dropped at the mouth of the Irrawaddy. The combination of para training and Gurkha bravery must have produced astounding warriors!

Special Forces

The Special Air Service was formed in the Middle East in October 1941. It and the Long Range Desert Group operated behind enemy lines. The 1st SAS Regiment was formed in 1942 and 2nd SAS in early 1943. They fought in Sicily and Italy and formed an SAS Brigade that, after D-Day, carried out many operations behind enemy lines.

ABOVE British SAS return after a three-month-long patrol, North Africa, 18 January 1943. Note the SAS breast pocket wings, the Arab shemagh and agal headdresses and the multitude of Vickers K .303in machine guns. The SAS was formed in July 1941 by David Stirling, who was captured on a mission in 1943 and ended up in Oflag IVC – Colditz Castle.

BELOW Men of No 4 Commando and paras of 6th Airborne Division in Bénouville on the east bank of the River Orne near what is today known as Pegasus Bridge, 6 June 1944. Commanded by Brigadier The Lord Lovat until he was wounded on 12 June, 1st Special Service Brigade fought in Normandy until September. Note the Combined Operations patch under the commando shoulder flash on the central corporal who carries a Browning M1911A1 pistol and a Bergen rucksack. The two glider men have Denison smocks, parachute trousers and helmets; the man to the left wears a battle jerkin. They are festooned with ammunition bandoleers.

In 1940 independent companies of army commandos were raised for the Norwegian campaign. Five were used, forming the nucleus of battalion-sized units carrying out hit-and-run raids in Europe. By March 1941 there were 12 battalions. In 1942 the first RM Commando was formed with a battalion strength of 24 officers and 440 ORs. The commandos proved their worth on D-Day and elsewhere. Postwar, the army commando battalions were disbanded and the Royal Marines took over.

Higher organisations

At the very top was the War Cabinet, below that the War Office and the Army Council. The latter had political and military members, the most senior military position being Chief of the Imperial General Staff (CIGS), the head of the British Army. Initially, when war broke out, Gen Sir Edmund Ironside (4 September 1939–26 May 1940) took over this seat from Lord Gort who was responsible for the BEF. After Ironside, FM Sir John Dill (until 25 December 1941) took over until he argued with Churchill. From December 1941 to the end of the war the position was held by Gen (later FM) Sir Alan Brooke. ❶

BELOW The overall
command of forces
in Britain came
under the GHQ UK
Forces. ❶ The country
was divided into various
command and districts
(see text). Canadian
forces in the UK came
under the Canadian
Army HQ. ❿
(All: RPJ Militaria)

Home Forces

These were controlled by the GOC Home Forces: Gen Sir Walter Kirke (until May 1940); Gen Ironside (to July 1940); Gen Alan Brooke (to December 1941); Gen Bernard Paget (to January 1944); then Gen Sir Harold Franklyn. The forces were divided into commands and districts, the most important being:

- Western Command (Lt Gen Sir Robert Haining), HQ Chester ❷
- Northern Command (Lt Gen Sir William Bartholomew), HQ York ❸
- Aldershot Command (Lt Gen Sir Charles Noel Frank Broad), HQ Aldershot, (renamed South Eastern Command in 1941 ❹; part of Southern Command from 1944 (various GOCs, HQ Tidworth) ❺
- Eastern Command HQ Luton Hoo from 1941 ❻
- Scottish Command HQ Edinburgh Castle ❼
- Northern Ireland District (Maj Gen Robert Pollok), HQ Belfast ❽
- London District (Maj Gen Andrew Thorne), HQ Horse Guards. ❾

Additionally, there was Anti-Aircraft Command (Lt Gen Sir Frederick Pile), HQ co-located with RAF Fighter Command at RAF Bentley Priory.

Home defence

Originally set up as the Local Defence Volunteers in May 1940 – mainly to bring some order to the ad hoc units that set themselves up as invasion became a possibility – the Home Guard has been immortalised by TV's *Dad's Army* and holds a special place in British hearts. Sir Anthony Eden broadcast on the BBC Home

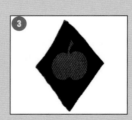

Armies consisted of two or more corps. These were raised by the British Army:

■ I Corps – part of the BEF, remained in UK based at Hickleton Hall, Northern Command until it took part in the assault on Normandy and battles in north-west Europe, during which time it came under First (Can) Army. ❶

■ I AB Corps – formed 1943, became part of 1st Allied AB Army in August 1944.

■ II Corps – after BEF, remained in UK based at Lower Hare Park, Newmarket, Eastern Command until disbanded early 1944. Involved in Operation Fortitude deception as part of fictitious Fourth Army. ❷

■ III Corps – after BEF, remained in UK based in Whitchurch, Shropshire, Western Command. Transferred to Persia and Iraq Command as part of the British Tenth Army. On 16 October 1944 it became HQ for Lt Gen Ronald Scobie during the Greek Civil War. On 17 December 1944 it was redesignated HQ Land Forces and Military Liaison (Greece). ❸

■ IV Corps – formed in Alresford, Hampshire, in February 1940 and from March to May 1940 fought in the Norwegian campaign under Lt Gen Claude Auchinleck. It commanded armoured reserves against the possible German invasion. Subsequently based near Northampton and then near Chesham where it was involved in training. In January 1942 the IV Corps HQ went to Iraq and, following the Japanese conquest of Burma, to India. As part of Fourteenth Army the corps – Indian 5th, 17th, 20th and 23rd Infantry divisions, Indian 50th Parachute Brigade and 254th Indian Tank Brigade – defeated the Japanese siege. In November 1944–February 1945 the corps advanced over the Irrawaddy and captured Meiktila. Reinforced by troops landed at the airfields near the town, it defended against Japanese counter-attacks during March. Reorganised, IV Corps – motorised 5th and 17th and the 19th Indian divisions with the 255th Tank Brigade – drove on Rangoon, after whose fall the corps was placed under the newly activated Twelfth Army to mop up. It was deactivated shortly after. ❹

■ V Corps – in Tidworth Camp within Southern Command, V Corps was commanded first by Lt Gen Claude Auchinleck and then Montgomery (22 July 1940–27 April 1941), when he was moved to XII Corps. V Corps took part in Operation Torch and the Tunisian campaign as part of the British First Army and the Italian campaign (British Eighth Army). ❺

■ VII Corps – formed in mid-1940 to counter the possible invasion, with 1st Canadian Infantry Division, 1st Armoured Division and 2nd New Zealand Expeditionary Force (UK), under the command of Canadian Lt Gen Andrew McNaughton. On 25 December 1940 it was renamed the Canadian Corps and based at Headley Court in Surrey. Reactivated as part of Operation Fortitude North, it was notionally disbanded in January 1945.

■ VIII Corps – part of UK Home Forces comprising 3rd and 48th (South Midland) divisions and, latterly, the 77th Infantry Division, it was based at Pyrland Hall near Cheddon Fitzpaine in Somerset. In 1944 and 1945 it was part of Second (BR) Army in Normandy and supported XXX Corps' east flank role during Operation Market Garden, captured Deurne and Helmond, and took part in the advance on Venray and Venlo. In 1945 it took part in Operation Plunder, crossed the Elbe and ended up in Plön in Schleswig-Holstein. ❻

(All: RPJ Militaria except 4 svg/WikiCommons)

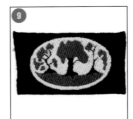

ABOVE Indian XV Corps was formed in 1942 in Bengal and fought through the war ending up taking Rangoon in an amphibious operation in 1945. *(RPJ Militaria)*

ABOVE Made up of Poles imprisoned in 1939 and freed from Russian captivity, Polish II Corps fought in Italy as part of British Eighth Army. *(RPJ Militaria)*

■ IX Corps – formed in April 1941 commanding 59th (Staffordshire) Infantry Division and the Durham and North Riding County Division followed by Northumberland County Division. The 15th (Scottish) Infantry Division transferred on 21 November 1941. The county divisions were disbanded and, on 1 December 1941, the corps was redesignated as IX Corps District. The 15th Division left on 28 September 1942, and the corps subsequently went to North Africa as the reserve for the Allied 18th Army Group on 24 March 1943. The 6th Armoured Division transferred to the corps on 12 March 1943 and it also took command of US 34th Infantry Division and part of the 46th Infantry Division. On 30 April British 7th Armoured and 4th Indian Infantry divisions joined, followed by the 201st Guards Brigade and the British 4th Infantry Division. With the Axis surrender in North Africa, IX Corps was run down and disbanded on 31 May 1943.

■ X Corps – formed in 1940 as part of UK Home Forces, it was based at Scotch Corner near Darlington within Northern Command. The corps moved to Syria and in summer 1942 joined the Eighth Army in Egypt to become a mobile corps, comprising 1st and 10th (BR) Armoured and 2nd New Zealand Infantry divisions. It played a major role at the Second Battle of El Alamein and the Tunisian campaign before joining Lt Gen Mark W. Clark's US Fifth Army to take part in the landings at Salerno, Italy, on 9 September 1943, where it comprised 46th and 56th (London) Infantry divisions and, later, 7th Armoured Division. It fought through Italy before the corps HQ was sent to Greece in late 1944. By March 1945 it had returned to Italy in reserve.

■ XI Corps was part of UK Home Forces, based at Bishop's Stortford in Hertfordshire. It was disbanded in July 1943.

■ XII Corps – formed in 1940 as part of UK Home Forces it was based in Royal Tunbridge Wells in Kent. Montgomery was its commander from 27 April 1941 to 13 August 1942. The corps went to Normandy in June 1944. One of its divisions – 59th (Staffordshire) Infantry Division – was broken up to reinforce other units, due to a severe shortage of manpower, in late August. XII Corps was on XXX Corps' west flank during Operation Market Garden and went on take part in Operations Pheasant and Blackcock before expanding east into Germany after Operation Plunder.

■ XIII Corps – on 1 January 1941 the Western Desert Force – British 7th Armoured Division, Australian 6th Infantry Division and 4th Indian Infantry Division – was redesignated XIII Corps. After the surrender of the Italian Tenth Army, XIII Corps HQ was deactivated until 14 April when it was reactivated as Western Desert Force HQ, becoming XIII Corps again in September 1941 as part of the new British Eighth Army. It took part in the invasion of Sicily in July 1943, the invasion of Italy on 3 September 1943, and fought with Eighth Army until 17 August 1944, when it transferred to Fifth (US) Army. Rejoining Eighth Army on 18 January 1945, it fought through to Trieste, holding it to mid-1946.

■ XXX Corps – fought as part of Eighth Army in the North African and Tunisian campaigns and the Allied invasion of Sicily before returning to the UK to prepare for the invasion of Normandy. It fought through north-west Europe from Normandy to the Baltic.

Manpower shortages

Infantry are always at the sharp end of the land battle, and infantry casualty rates during the Second World War were shockingly high. After the trenches of the First World War, everyone assumed that the next war – a war of mobility – would prove cheaper in terms of losses. How wrong they were. During the battles in Normandy casualties reached similar levels to those of the First World War, so much so that all the combatants had problems. The Germans devastated their replacement system when their losses in 1944–45 forced the mobilisation of entire training units, sometimes the instructors, too. The British and Canadians in particular suffered from severe manpower shortages and had to take extreme courses of action to overcome this: Operation Goldflake brought Canadian and British units to north-west Europe from Italy; a number of units – such as

BELOW A chaplain gives absolution to a dying Canadian soldier during the attack on Caen in July 1944. Note the CCS (Canadian Chaplain Service) in the divisional patch. The CCS was well respected by the troops. As Maj C.P. Stacey, the official historian of the Canadian Army put it, 'The fashion in which the chaplains have won the regard of the men by sharing the hardships and perils that fall to them was strikingly illustrated at Dieppe, where one chaplain was decorated and one mentioned in dispatches for bravery in succouring the wounded under fire, and a third, after working for hours among the casualties on the fire-swept beach near the casino, chose to remain with the wounded men and became a prisoner of war.'

ABOVE The 78th (Battleaxe) Division was one of the British Army's best, fighting from Operation Torch in 1942 through Sicily and Italy. Its 11th Brigade included the 2nd Lancashire Fusiliers, seen here alongside Achilles 17pdr tank destroyers, waiting to go advance on 22 April 1945, close to the end of the campaign.

BELOW HM LCI(L)-125 was commissioned into the Royal Navy through Lend-Lease and, manned by a Canadian crew, delivered A Coy, and 1st Pl, D Coy of the Highland Light Infantry of Canada onto Nan White Beach at high tide on D-Day. These were follow-up troops of 9th Inf Bde, the reserve brigade. Here, the port-side gangway is deployed allowing the men and their bicycles to disembark. (See also p. 141.) Note the waterproofing used by some soldiers to protect their rifles.

the 50th and 59th (BR) Infantry divisions – were broken up and their personnel sent to reinforce other units. Finally, Montgomery was careful to husband his infantry where he could, modifying his tactics and reducing his commitments wherever possible.

Stephen Hart relates:

The senior German commanders facing 21st Army Group during the campaign deduced the existence of casualty-conscious motivations behind Montgomery's utilisation of an attritional approach based on massive firepower. On 10 July 1944 General Gehr von Schweppenburg, commanding Panzer Gruppe West, astutely observed that:

'The British and Canadian troops were magnificent. . . . However . . . the command . . . was not making the best use of them. The command seemed slow and rather pedestrian. It seems that the Allied intention was to wear down their enemy with their enormous material superiority. It will never be known whether Montgomery had received private instruction from his Government to avoid for the British troops another bloodbath such as they had suffered in the First World War on the Somme and at Passchendaele.'

To postwar commentators, without knowledge of 21st Army Group's manpower problems, this concern about infantry shortages led to what was often seen as Montgomery's caution. Others remark on British and American over-reliance on artillery and tentativeness in attack; some, such as the US author Carlos d'Este, even go as far as to suggest the shortages were a myth caused by War Office inefficiencies.

In fact, it is indisputable that as the number of people required to keep soldiers in the field blossomed during the Second World War – an infantry division of 17,000 men only put 4,000 into the field – so much of the casualty burden fell increasingly on the few: the infantry, armour, engineer and field artillery units at the front. John Ellis, in his essential analysis of combat in the Second World War, *At the Sharp End*, provides many examples of the sacrifices borne by the infantry, which are summarised here:

- By the end of the Battle of Normandy (July 1944) 15th (Scottish) Division had lost 5,354 men. Of the 52 officers killed, 43 were from the nine infantry battalions.
- 15th (Scottish) Division then suffered 2,860 battle casualties from 13 September to 15 November 1944. Of these, 2,562 (89.6%) were from the ranks of the same nine infantry battalions.
- In the street fighting at Ortona in December 1943, a brigade of the 1st Canadian Division lost 1,372 casualties: a quarter of all Canadian deaths in Italy happened in this town.
- Between 9 September and 31 October 1943, the 5th Sherwood Foresters suffered 650 battle casualties, 9th Royal Fusiliers 572 and 5th Hampshire Regiment 448.
- By the end of the Battle of Normandy 3rd Infantry Division, which had landed on D-Day, had suffered 7,100 casualties, 904 of whom had been killed.
- During the Reichswald fighting, 53rd (Welsh) suffered 5,000 casualties in nine days.

In particular the officers suffered. Ellis compares British officer and OR casualties in four units in north-west Europe, 1944–45, in the following table:

COMPARISON BETWEEN OFFICER/OR HIT SURVIVABILITY				
Unit	% Hit		% Killed	
	Offr	ORs	Offr	ORs
50th (Northumbrian) Division	65.9	50.0	16.5	8.7
15th (Scottish) Division	72.2	62.9	28.7	16.8
6th KOSB	67.5	62.5	17.5	8.9
1/Norfolk	72.1	64.5	17.4	17.0
1/Dorset	70.6	62.0	25.9	13.2

Added to these battle casualties, 8.8% of Commonwealth losses were due to capture. That accounts for 38.21% of British and Commonwealth losses. This highlights the significant losses that occurred in 1939–42

(France, Hong Kong, Malaya and Singapore, the Desert War).

Unsurprisingly, all these losses were hard to sustain and reinforcement was not helped by miscalculations. Stephen Hart again:

The infantry reinforcement crisis of 1944 was, therefore, a long-term problem which was undoubtedly exacerbated by the War Office's underestimation of infantry casualty wastage rates. The War Office estimation of total casualties for all branches in the campaign's first six months was actually far higher than the figure actually suffered; 109,296 casualties suffered up to 12 December 1944 against a predicted figure of 171,855 casualties up to 5 December. However, predicted infantry casualties were far lower than actual wastage. 21st Army Group incurred 39,107 casualties by 1 September 1944, compared with 33,348 predicted casualties. . . .

The War Office had miscalculated the proportion that infantry casualties represented of total casualties incurred over all branches. The February 1944 casualty projection had estimated that infantry casualties would be between 38 per cent and 45 per cent of total casualties, depending on how widely infantry was defined. This estimate proved to be far too low. Infantry casualties within Canadian forces up to 17 August 1944 amounted to 76 per cent of total casualties.

The Canadian attrition continued into autumn: 1st Canadian Army's War Establishment in infantry other ranks was 20,599. On 2 September 1944, its deficit in infantry other ranks peaked at a staggering 19.2 per cent – some 3,917 soldiers. By 7 October 1944 the infantry other ranks deficit was still running at 10.69 per cent.' And to make matters worse, the Canadians had over 100,000 men – the so-called Zombies – sitting in Canada who refused to serve overseas.

While this survey has concentrated on Europe, the losses in other theatres were similarly bad and these were compounded by terrain difficulties for casualty evacuation and medical treatment (see Chapter 7).

ABOVE In July 1944, the Allied airborne troops were formed into the 1st Allied Airborne Army, under US Gen Lewis H. Brereton.
(RPJ Militaria)

ABOVE The badge worn by personnel of SHAEF, the Supreme Headquarters Allied Powers in Europe, commanded by Gen Dwight D. Eisenhower.
(RPJ Militaria)

1940 – quotas of recruits had been imposed on areas and operated by District Commissioners through Native Authorities. When formal conscription began in Tanganyika, 'most of the male population of Bagamoyo took to the bush' and 'were afraid they would be impressed if they came near the town', while in Dar es Salaam tax defaulters were conscripted.

Compulsory Service Regulations were imposed on West Africa in 1941 and Killingray identifies 10,000 conscripts raised including press-ganging. The unpopularity of service is well shown by the desertion rate: for example this stood at 42% of all Ashantis and 20% of all Gold Coast conscripts. Unpalatably, forced labourers in Tanganyika lived on guarded compounds to reduce desertion levels and corporal punishment was used. It is unlikely that was an isolated incident. Not all conscription was for military service: opencast tin mines in Nigeria; farm labour in Rhodesia – there were many labour requirements and the workers received very little in compensation for their work.

Called up

Having received his call-up papers, the first requirement for any conscript was to pass the medical test, administered by Civilian Medical Boards. They classified the recruit into one of four categories:

A – fit for general service at home and abroad
B – unfit for general service abroad but fit for base or garrison service at home and abroad
C – fit for home service only
D – unfit for any form of military service.

RIGHT The Soldier's Record and Paybook – Army Book 64 – carried personal details: soldier's name, description and attestation; particulars of training; leave warrants and record of uniform grant; medical classification, inoculations, vaccinations and dentures supplied. There were two parts: Part I was carried at all times; Part II fitted in the pocket at the back and was only issued and carried during wartime. It also recorded pay. *(RCT)*

This test – there were about 7 million of them during the war – didn't make allowances for where the recruit would go or what he would do and, therefore, wasn't fit for purpose as far as the forces were concerned. So, in 1940 a new system was introduced with more categories: A1, A2, B1, B2, B3, B4, B5, C, D, E (where C = home service only, D = temporarily unfit and E = permanently unfit). The categories were based on physical endurance, the ability to march, vision (in relation to shooting and driving), disease or illness that would affect military service and any problems that might affect the tasks that could be performed or locations visited – *eg* fit but couldn't visit the tropics.

The classification system never worked very well – as much anecdotal evidence attests – and by 1945 had over 70 sub-categories.

There was a better system, Canadian, known by its acronym PULHEMS where P = physical capacity, U = upper extremity, L = locomotion, H = hearing, E = eyesight, M = mental capacity, S = stability of emotions. The method was explained by Brig J.C. Meakins, Deputy Director General of Medical Services (Canadian Army) in an article in November 1943 and this quote exemplifies the thinking behind it:

Thirdly, must be considered locomotion (L). This has been in the past the principal criterion for a first-class soldier, which is exemplified by the primary requirement in past standards that a recruit must be able to march so many miles, walk so many miles, or be out. This was an arbitrary and unrealistic standard without consideration for the soldier's other functions. It reminds one of the occasion when a famous British regiment of foot were transformed into motorized infantry, and after a year of strenuous active service they were ordered to undertake a route march. There was almost a mutiny. 'They were damned if they would, as they hadn't walked for two years.' Quite rightly! They were wonderful motorized troops, knew their job and did it magnificently, so why walk? Flat feet, varicose veins, or what have you below the waist, are of little importance in a jeep or any other vehicle as long as it gets the infantry there and brings the enemy back. This example cannot be taken in its full implication,

but points a moral to adorn a tale that every soldier does not need perfect locomotion.

Adopted by the British Army during the war, it is still – with slight modifications – used today. Meakins also stressed that every job in the army needed to be analysed and aggregated into a category, and that officers of the Directorate of Personnel Selection 'should be on an equally high professional level as those of the Medical corps'. Having passed the medical, the conscript received a train warrant and instructions to report for initial training – six weeks of regimentation, kit inspections and bed-making, army food, square-bashing and rifle drill, and, of course, sergeant majors. For many 18-year-olds who hadn't left home before, this would have been a traumatic experience.

They would be issued with their uniforms – one conscript remembers two battledress uniforms, an overcoat, respirator, rifle, bayonet, denims, two pairs of boots . . . and then pay a visit to the barber. Then it was drill, training, inoculations, PE and more drill before another rail warrant would take the young soldier to his posting complete with kitbag and, sometimes, rifle. The conscript was in the army for the foreseeable future, and many wouldn't see home for a long time.

Training

All armies need to train. Some need more training than others. The German Army benefited from the general militarisation of German society: schools, the *Hitlerjugend* – Hitler Youth (HJ) – and RAD prepared young men for the army, physically and educationally. By the time German youths joined the *Wehrmacht* (German armed forces), their training period as conscripts could move very rapidly through the preliminary stages; in two or three months they could take part in manoeuvres and learn higher-level tactics.

The British, on the other hand, had nothing similar: the Boy Scout movement was hardly the equivalent of the HJ. This meant that when the Military Training Act required all British men aged 20 and 21 to take six months' military training and, subsequently, the National Services (Armed Forces) Act made men aged 18–41 liable for conscription, the army increased quickly in size but it wasn't full of hardened young men already used to physical work, regimentation and military discipline.

The British Army of the time consisted of a cadre of regulars swelled by the Territorial Army that had been doubled in size to 340,000 men from 29 March 1939. Along with the conscripts this meant that the total army strength when war was declared was 897,000 (as compared to France's 5 million and Germany's 3,737,000 plus 35,000 SS-VT). Conscription meant that the numbers rose to 1,128,000 by year's end. The regulars and TA provided the BEF, which was sent to France in September 1939, home defence and was also spread around the globe providing the controlling elements and backbone of British imperial power. Initial reverses reduced the size of the army. The fighting in Norway and France lost around 70,000 men – it could have been a lot worse had it not been for the around 370,000 evacuated. The losses included significant numbers of heavy weapons and many of the army's most experienced and competent soldiers. Take as an example the original 51st Highland Division: most were lost in battle or were numbered among the 10,000 captured at Saint-Valery-en-Caux in 1940.

These losses left Britain's defences – on paper at least – seriously weakened, although in fact German naval losses in the Norwegian campaign meant any cross-Channel operation would have been likely to fail. Initially, the defence of Britain was assisted by the arrival of the Canadian Army while the newly conscripted British troops were trained. It's important to remember just how many of the post-Dunkirk campaigns were considerably aided by Commonwealth and Dominion troops, who fought alongside Britain.

The British Isles swiftly became a training ground and this would only increase as the US Army built up in numbers from 1942, and in particular as the cross-Channel invasion neared. As well as the better-known areas – Salisbury Plain, Bovington and Lulworth, Kirkudbright and Castlemartin, and Armagh where many Americans trained – there were, literally, hundreds of others: 50 in Scotland alone from Achnacarry where the Commando Basic Training Centre could be found, to

HMS *Brontosaurus* based in Castle Toward at Dunoon where No 2 Combined Training Centre taught methods of loading and unloading landing craft (No 1 CTC was in Inveraray).

Directorate of Military Training and the Royal Army Educational Corps

Abolished in 1916, the Directorate of Military Training was re-established in 1927 and by the outbreak of war was responsible for tactical and technical training. The director was assisted by three Deputy Directors of Military Training, the Director of Technical Training, Major General Armoured Training and Major General Royal Artillery Training. There was also the Royal Army Education Corps, with the Director of Army Education responsible for education throughout the army. He was assisted by two deputy directors: General and Technical, the latter taking over many of the functions of the Deputy Director of Military Training (Technical). The Director, Army Bureau of Current Affairs was responsible for the preparation and publication of teaching aids. Interestingly, the RAEC played a fundamental role in the political education of armed forces personnel. From 1943 serving soldiers were supposed to receive 'citizenship education', which took the form of booklets and discussion periods. The material was collected together in one volume, *The British Way and Purpose* (1944). These discussions about postwar society, added to political lectures in the run-up to the 1945 General Election, played a role in the Labour Party's victory.

ABOVE Training for D-Day took place all over the UK from Scotland – Inveraray's No 1 Combined Training Centre (CTC) trained on minor landing craft such as LCAs; nearby, HMS *Brontosaurus*, No 2 CTC, provided training in the use of major landing craft such as LCTs – to large beach-landing exercises along the south coast of England. At Studland Bay, for example, Exercise Smash included bombing practice and live firing.

THE BRITISH WAY AND PURPOSE (BWP)

Produced by the RAEC, this was a series of booklets that educated the British Army personnel on a range of 'citizenship' issues. Produced 1942–44 and finally collected together in one book, the BWP did much to stimulate debate among the soldiers and helps partially to explain why the popular war leader Winston Churchill lost his mandate in 1945. The booklets were titled:

SOLDIER-CITIZEN

1 *Citizen of Britain* (A.D.K. Owen), November 1942
2 *Britain in Action*, December 1942
3 *Citizen of Empire*, January 1943
4 *Citizen of the World*, February 1943
5 *Review*, March 1943

REPORT ON THE NATION

6 *The Setting* (C.B. Fawcett), April 1943
7 *The Responsible Citizen* (Barbara Ward and A.D.K. Owen), May 1943
8 *The Citizen at Work*, June 1943
9 *The Home of the Citizen* (Elizabeth E. Halton), July 1943
10 *The Health of the Citizen* (F.A.E. Crew), August 1943
11 *Education and the Citizen* (E.S. Roberts and T.R. Weaver), September 1943
12 *What More Is Needed of the Citizen?* (A.D. Lindsay Page), October 1943

TODAY AND TOMORROW

13 *The Family and Neighbourhood*, December 1943
14 *People at Work* (H.A. Marquand), January 1944
15 *Britain in Europe*, February 1944
16 *You and the Empire*, March 1944
17 *You and the Colonies* (Sir William McLean), April 1944
18 *Britain and the Peace* (W. Arnold-Forster), May 1944

To find out more, the complete text is available at: https://archive.org/details/in.ernet.dli.2015.100180/page/n1/mode/2up)

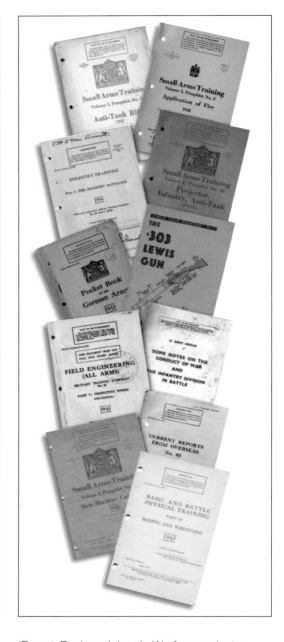

ABOVE RIGHT A selection of the many manuals – mainly produced by the War Office – to train the troops. However, not all of them were official: the Lewis Gun manual was published by Gale and Polden. Note Montgomery's *Notes on the Conduct of War* and *The Infantry Division in Battle*. (RCT)

Manuals

To help with the practical side of military training – provided by training bodies, officers and NCOs to their men not just in Britain but throughout British territories – there were various forms of written instruction which were amended and altered as events dictated. The War Office produced a set of Military Training pamphlets covering subjects as disparate as 'The Offensive' (No 2) and 'The Defence' (No 3) to '2-inch Mortar' (No 14), 'Drill for Foot Guards and Infantry of the Line' (No 18), 'Training in Fieldcraft and Elementary Tactics' (No 33),

'Forest, Bush and Jungle Warfare against a Modern Enemy' (No 52), 'Warfare in the Far East' (No 52) or 'Mountain Warfare' (No 56).

It's worth pointing out (as does Dr Timothy Harrison Place in his detailed survey *Military Training in the British Army, 1940–1944: From Dunkirk to D-Day*) that the process of producing these pamphlets wasn't always as swift as it should have been. He cites the two-year gestation of the *Infantry Training Part VIII Fieldcraft, Battle Drill, Section and Platoon Tactics*, which started in April 1942 and appeared in March 1944. However, there were other instruction pamphlets that appeared more regularly, such as the *Army Training Memorandum* sequence. These were initially produced monthly and sent to 'every officer in the British Army . . . by the third week of the month'. This soon became more sporadic and 29 were produced in total during the war. A typical contents listing (this is No 40 of August 1941) included: 'Know How to Shoot: Experience in Crete again shows the value of accurate rifle shooting . . .'; 'Unditching of Tanks: Infantry sub-units must always be on the look-out to assist tanks . . .'; 'Bangalore Torpedoes and Cordex Nets: Tests have been carried out with 2-in Bangalore torpedoes against German Teller (anti-tank) mines . . .'; 'Points to Examine in Unit Administration for Inspecting Officers . . .' and 'Developments in German Weapons: German Assault Artillery . . .'. Alongside a detailed appendix on 'Air Actions against Land Forces' was the more prosaic 'Guide to Officers' Kit' (see box on page 96).

Other pamphlets included *Army Training Instructions* – 'The co-operation of infantry and tanks' was ATI No 2 of May 1943, 'The organisation, training and employment of snipers', No 9 of April 1944 and 'Flame throwers' No 10 of July 1944. The battle experience titles *Notes from the Theatres of War* and *Current Reports from Overseas* were produced from 1942 and covered operations in specific areas such as Cyrenaica (eastern Libya) and Russia. The former – there were 21 produced, including 3 on the campaign in North Africa – according to Harrison Place 'represented the "official" lessons of battle experience . . . generally distributed one to each company or equivalent'. There were 96 of the latter and they did not provide accepted doctrine but simply examined the experiences. They were restricted in circulation to senior officers and covered such subjects as: 'Operations by a battalion of Canadian infantry in the valley of the River Laison', 'Notes on tactical handling of Wasps' and 'Statements by prisoners after capture of Le Havre' (No 60 of 25 October 1944) and the 'Japanese defence of Peleliu' and 'A waterborne raid over the Waal' (No 92 of 20 June 1945). Interestingly, these were not always without censorship – Harrison Place quotes Montgomery's removal

from After Action reports of an assessment that equated the superiority of the Tiger and Panther over the Sherman and Cromwell to the position in the desert when the British Crusaders and Honeys (M3 Stuarts) were outclassed by the German PzKpfw IIIs and IVs.

It wasn't just direct military subjects that were covered: physical training was also an important topic. The 'Battle and Physical Training' series of 1945 replaced *Purposeful and Basic Physical Training* of 1942 with 11 parts covering:

I.   General principles of basic and battle physical training and methods of instruction.
II. Basic physical training tables and basic physical efficiency tests.
III. Syllabus of battle physical training and battle physical efficiency tests.
IV. Endurance training.
V.   Jumping, vaulting, climbing, scaling and obstacle training.
VI. Pulling, pushing, lifting and carrying.
VII. Throwing, balancing, mountaineering and ski exercises.
VIII. Swimming, life saving and improvised aids to crossing water obstacles.
IX. Boxing and wrestling.
X.   Shoot to kill (physical training for weapon training).
XI. Team games and recreational training.

In the end, official booklets and pamphlets played an important educational role, although there was a lot of reading involved and many couldn't find time for this with all their other duties.

There were many people who wanted instructional pamphlets, some of them for operational reasons: the Home Guard, for example, which was announced on 14 May 1940, when the Secretary of State for War, Anthony Eden, made a radio broadcast asking all men aged 17–65 and not in the forces to sign up to become Local Defence Volunteers. While militarily of dubious value, it was necessary to create such an organisation to ensure some sort of control over the groups that had sprung up since the start of the war, the numbers increasing since the fall of France.

As a morale booster it was important – and continues to be if the repeats of *Dad's Army* are anything to go by! The numbers enlisting were three times greater than the 500,000 anticipated and immediately presented the authorities with a challenge. To provide uniforms, weapons

FIELD SERVICE POCKET BOOK

Issued 'on a pool basis, the distribution to the unit being sufficient to permit of an issue down to serjeants . . . Territorial Army units will receive the same distribution as regular units', this set of pamphlets came out in 1939 and was updated through the war. They built up into a reference and provided suggestions for 'instructional exercises in connection with operations'.

The first issue – found today in book form and also with a sturdy clip-fastening – identified the following potential content:

1 Glossary of Military Terms and Organization in the Field.
2 Orders and Intercommunication.
2A The T Panel Code.
3 Intelligence – Information and Security.
4 Field Engineering.
5 Billets, Camps and Bivouacs. Camp Cooking and Water Arrangements.
6 Mechanised Movement by Road.
7 Movement by Sea, Air and Rail.
8 Defence Against Gas.
9 Supply and Replenishment of Material in the Field.
9A Ammunition Abbreviations.
10 Medical Services.
11 Discipline, Office Work and Burial Parties.
12 Miscellaneous Tables and Data.
13 Notes For a Staff Officer.

Subsequently in 1943–44 revised titles were introduced
Part I 1   Glossary of Military Terms.
Part I 3   Abbreviations.
Part I 3A   Ammunition Abbreviations.
Part I 4   Appreciations, Orders, Messages and Intercommunication.
Part II 4A Staff Organization and Staff Duties in the US Army
Part I 5   Signal Codes.
Part II 5   Movement by Road and Rail.
Part I 6   Intelligence – Information and Security.
Part II 6   Administration
Part I 6A   Conventional Military Symbols.
Part I 7   Field Engineering.
Part I 9   Movement by Road and Rail.
Part I 10   Gas.
Part I 12   First Aid and Hygiene.
Part I 13   Discipline, Office Work, Pay, and Burial Parties

and training – all of which were essential if the force was to have any credibility – required a significant effort and, in mid-1940, that was a problem. Step in the commercial publishers such as Nicholson & Watson (*Know Your Weapons series, No 1 Tommy Gun*) and Gale & Polden of Aldershot (*The Sten Machine Carbine*; *The Bren Light Machine Gun Description, Use and Mechanism*; *Boys Anti-Tank rifle Mark I*; *Lewis Gun Mechanism made easy*; *Browning Heavy Machine Gun Mechanism made easy*, etc). The latter printed its first book, on the Franco-Prussian War, in 1873. Others included Barnards Ltd (*Manual of Rifles/Small Arms and Special Weapons/Modern Automatic Guns*). Home Guard, air defence volunteers and many small boys were happy to discover the finer points of many subjects from aircraft recognition to weapons.

Training centres and schools

Before 1939, basic training – four months of it – took place at one of the 64 regimental depots but these couldn't cope with the influx of new conscripts. The Infantry Training Centres (ITCs) were created but it soon became obvious that training wasn't reaching desired levels. Peter Johnston's blog quotes Maj Gen J.S. Nicols' 'State of Training of Reinforcements' of 21 September 1942: 'In September 1942, of 860 reinforcements posted to the 50th Division, Eighth Army, only one quarter had done any field firing at all, seven had never previously fired a rifle, nine had never fired a Bren gun, 131 had never thrown a live grenade and 138 had never fired a Thompson submachine gun!' From 1942 the system changed. All new recruits joined the General Service Corps under whose aegis basic training took place at Primary Training Centres or the Primary Training Wings of ITCs. Once complete, the conscripts chosen for the infantry went to ITCs for a further ten weeks of training (this could be increased for specialists – anti-tank gunners, signallers, etc). By 1944 nearly 200,000 men were in PTCs or ITCs.

Officer training

Two pre-OCTU schools were set up to bring the candidates up to a uniform standard of knowledge and the Highland Fieldcraft Training

Centre (closed 1944) was formed to develop character and well-being. Pre-OCTU stays lasted from two to eight weeks. Over 100,000 potential officers went through OCTUs, originally selected based on a CO's recommendation followed by an interview (something that led to accusations of class bias). From April 1942 the War Office Selection Board took over, leading to more socially mobile candidates. It's worth noting that during the war, the number of regular officers totalled 14,000 while nearly 250,000 were commissioned for the duration of hostilities.

After the OCTUs, officers went to the GHQ Home Forces Battle School at Barnard Castle, where physical pressure induced levels of stress that replicated the pressure of combat as far as it was possible to do so. The level of training at battle schools in general was mixed but at least one Canloan officer described the course at Barnard Castle as 'the most efficient, imaginative and thorough educational experience of my lifetime'. Chief instructor there was Lionel Wigram (1907–44) who, as Tim Harrison Place comments, 'played a leading part in spreading [Battle Drill] to the whole of the Home Army'. He did so by training instructors who would teach at the divisional battle schools set up in each infantry division as ordered by General Sir Bernard Paget when he became GOC of GHQ Home Forces. The exemplar was the 47th Division School of Battle Drill, which opened in July 1941 in South-Eastern Command (where Paget was, at the time, GOC before taking on the Home Forces appointment in December 1941).

At the end of 1942 the School of Infantry was set up at Barnard Castle (Battle School became a wing) teaching platoon commanders (28 days), company commanders (21 days) and COs' courses (21 days). The instructors started out with less experience than some of the men attending, but by war's end experienced soldiers were used as teachers.

The School of Infantry moved to its current home in Warminster in 1945, amalgamating with the NCOs' school. There was also a Small Arms School in Hythe with a snipers' wing at Bisley. The SAS taught use of most small arms: 2in mortar, PIAT, Sten, grenades, Vickers MMG and 20mm AA gun. The Infantry Heavy Weapons School was the Netheravon Wing of

PRIMARY TRAINING CENTRES

ITC	Location	Associated unit
1	Warley	RF, Essex
2	Norwich	Norfolk, Northamptons
3	Bury St Edmunds	Suffolk, Bedfs Herts
4	Brancepeth	Dukes, DLI
5	Richmond	EYorks, Green Howards, Manch
6	Strensall	WYorks, LF, KOYLI
7	Lincoln	Lincolns, Foresters, Y&L
8	Perth	Black Watch, A&SH
9	Aberdeen	Camerons, HLI, Gordons
10	Berwick	RS, RSF, KOSB
11	Fort George	Seaforth, Camerons
12	Canterbury	Buffs, Surreys
13	Maidstone	Queen's, RWK
14	Dorchester	Devons, DCLI, Dorset
15	Gloucester	Som LI, Glosters, Wilts
16	Oxford	Hamps, OxfBucks
17	Reading/Colchester (moved in January 1943)	RBerks, RSussex
18	Carlisle	King's Own, Border, Loyals
19	Formby	King's, ELanR, PWV
20	Shrewsbury	NStaffs, KSLI
21	Brecon	RWF, SWB, Welch
22	Warwick	Warwick, Leicesters
23	Worcester	WorcR, SStaffords
24	Chester	NF, Cheshire, Middlesex Regt, Manch
25	Ballykinler	RInnisks, RUR, RIrF
1 MTB	Chiseldon/Strensall (moved in autumn 1942, disbanded 1943)	KRRC
2 MTB	Ranby	RB

the SAS where the .303 Vickers MMG and the 3in mortar were taught, as were, after 1942, the 2pdr and 6pdr anti-tank guns and, from October 1942, 4.2in mortars.

Battle Drill

Early in the war, while there were so many men to train and so few instructors with any experience, the tendency was to produce drills for all tactical situations. This policy initially served its purpose in that it enabled students to be taught to do something rather than nothing when faced with a problem. The 47th Division's improved Battle Drill training method, however, raised enthusiasm

THE RATIONALE FOR BATTLE DRILL

'The place of the infantryman in the symphony of war.

'William Shirer in his recent book *Berlin Diary* said (about the German Army): "The gulf between officers and men is gone in this war. The German Officer no longer represents – a class or caste. All the men in the ranks feel this. They feel like members of one great family." In short the Reichswehr – Holy of holies of military tradition, formality and diehardism, has deliberately cast all these things aside in the interests of better war-making.

'Hard indeed must it be for us to learn such lessons as co-operation and team work from a nation of sportsmen as rotten as the Huns. But facts must be faced. They are making us look third rate in war just as they did in the Olympic Games, not because their individual man is better than ours, but because their system of selecting the men, of training them to produce the team, and their understanding of the sort of team that is needed to win – is so much better than ours.

'We are still far behind in these fields. We have at last realised that to win this war, Bren Guns, 3-inch Mortars, Tanks, Planes and Guns are necessary. But have we realised that MEN are necessary – men with knowledge and skill to co-ordinate the use of all these intricate weapons?

'Tanks, planes and guns, and the men who work them, have certainly contributed in no small measure to the German victories. But it is always overlooked that the infantry have played just as big a part in the game – highly trained, methodically practised, skilled fighting men – always nipping in with that little extra effort at the right place, and at the right time.

'The individual infantryman of to-day to do his job well must be a star individual performer. He will never develop his skill if he is to be regarded as a casual labourer who can learn all there is to know about the job in a few weeks of so-called training. The individual Infantryman of Britain has all the talents. He could easily become that star performer. But he will never do so if he is expected to play an intricate piece of Brahms as the leading soloist in a large orchestra whose other members he is never allowed to know or see.

'To play that intricate piece well, he must have that practice – regular, methodical practice. He must have that practice ultimately not alone, but surrounded by his supporting colleagues all working together as members of one great harmonious band.

'He must have Battle Drill.'

Source: *Battle School*
(via www.vickersmg.org.uk)

immediately. Indeed, Wigram's syllabus included many things that could only be of benefit to its students: an emphasis on fieldcraft, small-unit tactics such as infiltration and pincer movements, night patrols, village fighting and house clearances. The drills were designed to simplify procedures and to speed up reaction time, and to ensure that all units had a similar baseline of tactics which would allow different units to work together in battle. It also emphasised vigorous physical action – something that Montgomery particularly liked – and live firing. This was contentious only in as much as there were fatalities. More divisive, however, was the hate training, involving the objectification of the enemy – something definitely seen as un-British.

The exercises or 'drills' allowed sections and platoons to practise and become conversant with various tactical situations so that they would know what to do on the battlefield – but battle drill also had its detractors. It was felt by some that the drills tended to become the masters and not the servants, commanders being inclined to act blindly and without first appreciating the situation. They believed that learning drills by rote stifled initiative. The War Office was decidedly lukewarm about battle drill until Alan Brooke became CIGS and, shortly after, Maj Gen J.A.C. Whitaker became Director of Military Training. He immediately tasked Maj James Brind to revise the current infantry training manual. Brind's revision led to *Infantry Training Part VIII Fieldcraft, Battle Drill, Section and Platoon Tactics* (published in March 1944). This borrowed heavily from battle drill as a comparison of drill 2 ('House Clearing', see pages 67–69) shows. (Drill 1 shows the difference between the platoon weapon/ ammunition allocations in 1941 and 1944.)

Nevertheless, battle drill, for whatever reason, lost favour – not helped by the fact that Wigram left in May 1943 (he later died in Italy in February 1944) and his original instructors were also moved to other jobs. By summer 1944 Wigram's battle drill section at Barnard Castle had closed down. Timothy Harrison Place remarks that it was not too much battle drill that deprived the British infantry of the power of initiative, but too little.

1941

The infantry platoon

The platoon comprised an HQ and three sections. The section increased from 8 to 10 men during the war. It started with an officer and 29 men, increasing nominally to 36 men. It was rare for platoons to be at full strength in battle conditions. The Boys anti-tank team was made up from platoon personnel. 1941 info from Battle Drill. 1944 info from Infantry Training Part VIII.

Soldier	Weapon	Personal ammunition	Extras
Section commander	Tommy gun	6 mags each 20 rounds	Wire cutters
2IC Section 1	Rifle	50 SAA	3 Bren mags
No 1 on Bren LMG	Bren	3 mags	
No 2 on Bren LMG	Rifle	50 SAA	Utility pouches containing 6 Bren mags
			Spare parts wallet
			3 Bren mags in his own pouches
No.1 Rifleman	Rifle	50 SAA	4 grenades
No. 1 Bomber	Rifle	50 SAA	4 grenades
Smoke man	Rifle	50 SAA	4 smoke canisters, No 14, Mk 1
No. 2 Rifleman	Rifle	50 SAA	3 Bren mags
Platoon HQ			
Officer/Sergeant	Rifle	50 SAA	3 Bren mags
Runner	Rifle	50 SAA	Very pistol
			12 white, 6 red, 6 green flares
			3 Bren mags
Batman (only if officer)	Rifle	50 SAA	3 Bren mags
No 1 ATk	ATk Rifle	50 SAA	1 ATk mag (5 rounds)
No 2 ATk	Rifle	50 SAA	8 ATk mags in utility pouches
No 1 Mortar	Mortar	6 HE bombs	
No 2 Mortar	Rifle	50 SAA	6 HE smoke bombs

Notes

1. **Gas.** Some slight risk is taken, but this does not mean any relaxation of gas precautions. The risk of gas in confused mobile fighting of forward infantry is not as great as in the old trench warfare, because it would probably hamper the enemy rather than help them. Fieldcraft and fighting efficiency are greatly improved by this dress, so the risk is worth taking.

2. **Bren ammunition.** Each section has 21 magazines per Bren gun plus sufficient additional ammunition to fill a further 3 magazines. In addition there is in this drill a reserve of 9 magazines *moving* up with Platoon HQ.

3. Only 1 set of *utility pouches* is carried per section. These pouches are uncomfortable and tend to reduce speed and efficiency.

4. **Smoke canisters.** Most useful – are carried at the scale of 4 per section.

5. On a number of practice exercises with live ammunition against a typical platoon objective, the average ammunition expenditure has been about 3 or 4 mags per Bren gun and 3 to 6 HE mortar bombs. All students (including many with much practical experience of actual fighting) have agreed that the volume of fire produced by this expenditure would in their opinion be adequate to neutralise the post.

1944

Suggested weapons/ammunition carriage of an infantry platoon, 1944

	SAA			Sten			Bren			Mortar		
	Rifle	Rifle	Sten	Mags	SAA	Bren	Mags	SAA	Mortar	HE	Smoke	Grenades
Pl HQ												
Pl commander												
Pl sergeant	1	50										4
Mortar L/Cpl	1	50								3	9	
No 1 Mortar			1	5	160				1	3	3	
No 2 Mortar	1	50								6	6	
Runner	1	50										2
Batman	1	50										
(38 set if allocated)												
Total HQ	5	250	1	5	160				1	12	18	6
Rifle Sect												
Sect commander			1	5	160							2
No 1 Rifleman	1	50					2	56+50				1
No 2 Rifleman	1	50					2	56+50				1
No 3 Rifleman	1	50					2	56+50				1
No 4 Rifleman	1	50					2	56+50				1
No 5 Rifleman	1	50					2	56+50				1
No 6 Rifleman	1	50					2	56+50				1
Bren gun												
2IC	1	50					4	112				
No 1 Bren						1	4	112				
No 2 Bren	1	50					5	140				2
Total Sect	8	400	1	5	160	1	25	1,000				10
Total Pl	29	1,450	4	20	640	3	75	3,000	1	12	18	36

Notes: 3 sets utility pouches carried by mortar detachment in addition to their basic pouches.
2 sets utility pouches per section carried by 2IC and No 2 Bren additional to basic pouches.
Signal bombs as ordered will displace Smoke and HE.

10 grenades per section; 6 grenades HQ (36, 69, 77).
74 and 75 grenades are occasional weapons only to be carried when specially ordered.

What replaced it? That's the problem right there! The performance of British and Commonwealth forces in Normandy has been criticised for its apparent lack of tank/infantry coordination and generally sluggish tactics. The fault seems to have been Montgomery's, as his overall doctrine – to some extent forced upon him by strictures on manpower and the political necessity of retaining Britain's place in the Allied power structure – was to promote an artillery-led battle plan. While it is certainly true that there were obvious instances of poor tactical awareness in the Normandy campaign, and that the failure to close the Falaise Gap quickly saw the Canadians scapegoated for their slowness, it's important to recognise various contributing factors:

- the problems with terrain – the bocage – proved conducive to the defence and extremely difficult for the Allied attackers
- attrition and the sheer number of infantry casualties meant that both sides were guilty of tactical blunders: the German propensity to counter-attack often led to annihilation by artillery
- after the force buildu-p reached equality in Normandy, and space became too limited for a war of movement, the advantage was definitely with the defenders, even if the Allies had air superiority
- finally, as summed up well by Dr Ben H. Shepherd in *Iron Cross* magazine:
  During the Normandy campaign, the German frontline soldier proved a resourceful and obdurate enemy.

Indeed it has been claimed, albeit with some exaggeration, that he possessed double the fighting power of his British, American or Canadian opponents. His defensive combat performance was the culmination of years of technical, doctrinal and psychological evolution, a process that imbued him with immensely high levels of resilience and flexibility.

Yet it would be a mistake to succumb wholesale to an image of peerless fighting performance. For one thing it was never entirely true; for another, the German army's fighting performance was intertwined with its status as the main sword arm of a barbaric dictatorship. Anyone seeking to slight the military performance of the soldiers of western democracy compared with those of Nazi Germany would do well to remember this.

And, of course, if you had suggested to one of the British or Canadian soldiers toasting their Russian allies on the shores of the Baltic in the ruins of the Third Reich what they thought about German superiority, their answer would have been pithy, to say the least.

Exercises

The short period of early infantry training undergone by anybody who joins the services has been seized on by Hollywood as a significant rite of passage. We all know about spit and polish, assault courses and

CONTINUED ON PAGE 70

BELOW Exercise Fabius began on 2 May 1944 and provided six days of practice for the landings at Omaha (Fabius 1), Gold (2), Juno (3) and Sword (4). Two other exercises (5 and 6) practised logistics. Here, troops exit a Landing Craft Assault (LCA).

Drills for House Clearing

1941
Principles.

3. Houses will be cleared from the rear gardens so that any enemy attempting to escape are driven on to the killing ground.

4. Houses will be cleared from the TOP downwards. An enemy driven up higher and higher in a large building may become offensive as he is compressed and concentrated in a better and better fire position. An enemy driven downwards towards the cellars is getting continuously into a worse and worse fire position. He becomes very vulnerable to attack by grenade and will be very likely to surrender or to attempt to escape via the front door – DEATH.

BELOW Compare this to the same subject in 1944 (see box on p. 69). *(RCT)*

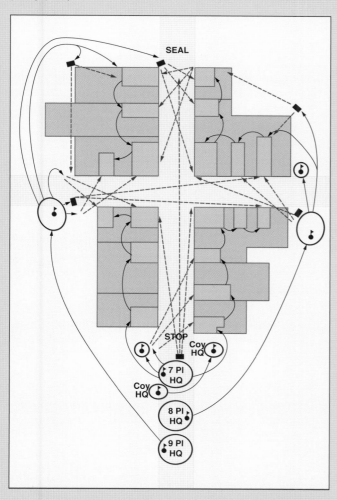

Drills for clearing a house

(N.B. – these also apply to the actual buildings of isolated farms and farm building groups – see drill for clearing a wood or isolated cover).

1 Divide section into:

Clearing group – Sec Comd and 3 men (1 Bomber under 2 doormen).

Covering group – Remainder under Section 2IC.

2 Covering group take up positions covering ALL windows, doors or openings which command the line of approach of the clearing party **to the back door** of the house.

3 Doormen approach the door covered by the Sec Comd (with Tommy Gun) and the covering group.

4 Left and right doormen kneel beside the door and open the latch with their bayonets, flinging the door wide open. During this operation the doormen keep their rifles on the outside of the body and have their fingers on the trigger. A doorman flings a grenade into the house if ordered to do so by the section commander.

Note: All the clearing group carry as many grenades as can be spared.

5 Sec Comd dashes in, followed closely by:

Bomber.

Left doorman.

Right doorman.

  (a) **The right doorman** glues his back to the hall wall near the door.

    Task. To cover the rear of the clearing party and prevent the free movement of the enemy downstairs, also to cover the cellar head.

  (b) **Remainder.** Go straight to the top of the house and clear it, working downwards from the roof (which must be searched) towards the cellars.

Notes

1. Don't get too grenade minded. It is very easy to get windy on this operation and fling grenades into every house or room for the sake of flinging them. They will soon run out and will not be available when really necessary.

2. SHOOT TO KILL. YOU CANNOT AFFORD TO TAKE CHANCES IN THIS SORT OF OPERATION.

3. Shooting through the walls of wooden buildings is useful but thorough personal search must follow it.

4. Search the front gardens of each house from the front upper windows before passing to the next house.

5. Don't worry about booby traps. A defended village (as distinct from an abandoned village) is unlikely to be booby-trapped. If it is you are not likely to find the traps – it takes an expert. So go right ahead and take risks – until something happens.

1944

By 1944 experience led to a more complete coverage (numbers below refer to paragraphs in *Infantry Training Part VIII Fieldcraft, Battle Drill, Section and Platoon Tactics*) note these are edited excerpts:

141. General

Fieldcraft does not apply to the open country alone. It must also be used in villages and towns. Villages and towns will probably be by-passed by leading troops and cleared later by troops specially detailed for the purpose. The clearance may be a costly undertaking and every man must know what he is doing and how to do it. A drill is therefore essential.

142. Probable enemy defensive measures

(a) All main streets will probably be barricaded or will have road blocks, but the barricade or road block, once captured, may provide cover for the fire section.

(b) It is probable that the outer perimeter of the village or parts of it will be strongly held. Covering groups must reply instantly to any fire that may come from houses of this kind, also to watch the roof tops which are a favourite hiding place for enemy snipers.

(c) It is a common German practice to defend the ground floor of a house strongly, retreating to the top story once an entry has been forced.

(d) Wire netting is often put over windows to deflect grenades. This should be carefully looked for.

(e) Doors will probably be locked or barricaded. If so, the door must be knocked down or blown open; otherwise entry must be made through a window, or by blowing a hole in a wall.

(f) In a defended room the enemy may erect a corner barricade. This can easily be improvised with furniture, and it will be grenade proof. Do not therefore jump to the conclusion that because your grenade has burst in a room all the enemy in that room have been killed. Look out for these barricades and have another grenade ready to throw behind them.

(g) The enemy sites his machine-gun and rifles well back from windows or holes in walls. Therefore enter the room at top speed.

(h) In a defended village only certain houses will be defended – the ones that occupy tactical positions. But every house must be searched, for it is fatal to leave a house behind you occupied by the enemy. Look out for 'mouseholing', the system by which the enemy makes holes in walls from house to house so that he can move down a terrace unhindered. This mouseholing may be in the cellar or concealed behind cupboards.

(i) It is unlikely that you will encounter booby traps in a defended village. Booby traps should be looked for in a village which has been abandoned by the enemy. It is possible, however, that even in a defended village, houses which are not themselves defended may have been booby trapped.

143. Principles

(a) Buildings will always, if possible, be cleared from the back gardens and yards, because these provide the best covered line of approach. Any enemy driven through the house out into the main street will thus be caught by the fire of the fire sections. When approaching the rear of buildings clear all outbuildings, sheds, and cover first. Never leave any uncleared building or outbuilding behind you. Make sure that your rear is clear before you move on.

(b) On entering buildings the ideal is to enter from the top and work downwards. If you have to enter from the ground floor, all efforts should be made to get to the top floor at once and to clear the house from the attic downwards. An enemy driven up higher and higher in a large building may become more offensive as he is driven into a tighter corner and to a better fire position. An enemy driven downwards towards cellars is getting continuously into a worse fire position. It is easier to throw a grenade downstairs than to throw upwards and it is very likely that an enemy driven downwards will feel tempted to escape into the main street. In a house which is very strongly defended it may not be possible to rush straight to the attic, though it should be attempted. If the attempt fails there is no alternative but to work slowly upwards by careful fire and movement.

144. Section drill for clearing a house

(i) Clearing group – Section commander, Bomber, First entry man, Second entry man, Look-out man. The section commander and bomber take up intermediate positions from which to direct and cover entry men towards the point of entry. Entry men approach the point of entry at best speed according to cover available. On gaining an entrance entry men get quickly away from the point of entry and stand with their backs to the wall covering the rest of the room and any doors. Section commander and bomber follow up entry men (as a result of observation or on signal from the latter). Look-out man remains at the entry. The remainder aim at getting to the top of the house as quickly as possible, leaving the second entry man near the entrance of the room to cover any stairs and passages. The house is searched downwards from the top.

(ii) Covering group – The Bren group with the remainder of the riflemen under the section 2IC. Follow up and if so ordered by the section commander enter the house as soon as the entry group have completed their entry. They will assist the second entry man in covering points from which the enemy may approach and, under the 2IC, will be prepared to help search the house or to provide fire outside the house

Platoon drill for clearing occupied houses

Plan [see diagram opposite and table below].
- No 1 section gives covering fire.
- No 2 section assaults houses on right.
- No 3 section assaults houses on left.
- Platoon HQ and reserve move forward one or two houses in rear of one or other leading sections. Part of platoon HQ may assist No 1 section in giving covering fire.
- Streets or back areas A and C are killing grounds and out of bounds to attackers.
- B may be used by attackers for speed of movement under overhead covering fire.

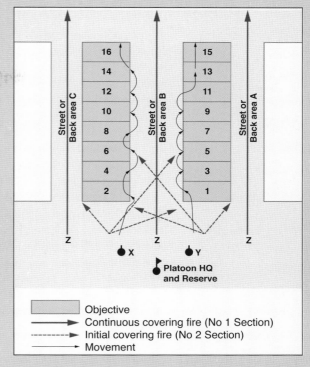

	Objective
⟶	Continuous covering fire (No 1 Section)
┄┄➤	Initial covering fire (No 2 Section)
⟶	Movement

No 1 Section (i) Siting of initial covering fire, and forming up assault sections	No 2 Section	No 3 Section	Pl HQ and Reserve
(ii) Covering fire	Clearing group assaults and clears House 1.	Covering fire	Covering fire and general direction of attack.
(iii) Covering fire	Covering group follow up clearing group as soon as latter have entered house successfully.	Covering fire	Covering fire
(iv) Covering fire	Section commander posts section to fire across on to House 1, and signals to No 3 section as soon as this covering fire is posted.	Covering fire	Covering fire
(v) Covering fire	Covering fire	Clearing group assaults and clears House 2.	Covering fire
(vi) Covering fire	Covering fire	Covering group follow up clearing group as soon as latter have entered successfully.	Covering fire
(vii) Covering fire	Covering fire	Section comd posts section to fire across House 3, and signals to No 2 section as soon as covering fire is posted.	Covering fire
(viii) Section moves forward as required to cover further advance of Nos 2 and 3 sections.	2 and 3 sections work alternately as above until moment when covering fire from No. 1 section is required further forward. Nos 2 and 3 sections can either continue simultaneously with forward move of No 1 section or cover its move until No 1 section in position.	Follow in rear of either Nos 2 or 3 sections when latter have reached (approx.) House 5 or 6.	

tough sergeant majors brutalising their young charges to ensure that boys become men who react in a cool military fashion when in action. However, what Hollywood doesn't say is that, in reality, when not actually fighting, most of service life is about training – in wartime more so than in peacetime. As well as improving and expanding knowledge, training and learning for promotion and familiarisation on new equipment, armies have to rehearse their forthcoming attacks, tactics and fieldcraft. They must improve continuously their weapons handling and shooting accuracy; their ability to react to the unexpected, how to cope with adversity and to manage success and exploit it fully. This sort of training may take the form of repetitive weapon stripping and cleaning, range and target shooting – or working on boarding and exiting landing craft. For officers it might involve Tactical Exercises Without Troops (TEWTS) or manoeuvres on one of the many training areas in Britain.

As D-Day approached, the skills training that took place in the smaller centres was subsumed in unit exercises that started small – such as the 2nd Ox and Bucks practising for Operation Deadstick, the coup de main operation against the bridges over the River Orne and Canal de Caen at Bénouville or 50th Infantry Division landing at Studland Bay in Exercise Smash (18 April 1944) – and ended up with two huge dress rehearsals for the main event: Exercise Tiger (22–30 April) for Force U, the American troops destined to land on Utah Beach; and Exercise Fabius (23 April– 7 May) for the other four beaches (the US troops on Omaha and British and Canadians on Gold, Juno and Sword). These tested the actual troops who would take part in the invasion in as close to actual battle conditions as possible, including live firing. Unfortunately, 'Tiger' saw practice become reality as German E-boats attacked one of the convoys in Lyme Bay and 749 died, and friendly fire also killed as many as 450 men.

Training in the field

Training is not something that ends once an army comes in contact with the enemy. Indeed, out of combat professional soldiers do what all professionals do: hone their skills.

For those conscripts who might not regard themselves as professionals, training would have reinforced the fact that they were and that their lives depended on professionalism. And, when they received them, newcomers had to be brought into the unit and, as the war went on, not all of them had had much training. Casualties for the infantry were numerous and replacements tended to come in groups. In *The Infantry Division in Battle*, FM B.L. Montgomery identified his key points for training in the field:

67. Training is preparation for battle. All training must therefore be realistic, and connected directly in a man's mind with his conduct in battle.

When troops first go into action, much will depend not only on the soundness of their training, but even more on their ability to carry out in battle what they have learnt in training.

68. There are plenty of opportunities for training in any theatre of war, but they are often of a fleeting nature. In order to derive the maximum benefit from such training it is absolutely essential that it shall be properly organized.

69. A small central Divisional School will pay a good dividend. Instructors must be carefully selected, preferably by the Commander personally, and they should be changed at frequent intervals.

Courses can be run to meet requirements as they vary from time to time.

It is no exaggeration to say that the success in battle depends greatly upon the ability of infantry junior leaders to lead and command. Casualties amongst these will always be high, and reinforcements will seldom contain a large enough proportion of them to fill the gaps.

Many private soldiers when they get into action will show the qualities of leadership, and short courses at the Divisional School will give them the necessary technical and tactical knowledge.

In additon NCOs who become 'rusty' can be sent for refresher courses, and lessons of the campaign as they are learnt can be incorporated in the courses, and thus spread amongst the junior ranks of all units.

Other courses might include training of battalion signallers, OP [observation post] parties from field regiments, Provost personnel, etc., to forestall shortages as they become probable.

Courses can be run for Arms such as the Divisional RE, to deal with technical developments.

Apart from its training side the Divisional School will be of great value in fostering the Divisional spirit and in providing a temporary change of atmosphere for officers and other ranks. They must be returned to their unit brimming over with enthusiasm.

The Divisional Commander should make this school his personal responsibility and pride.

70. It will at all times be possible to withdraw a Division for special training before a particular operation. This training should be dealt with in three stages:

(a) The individual and unit collective training of all Arms in the specialized requirements of the particular operation, i.e. assault boating for the crossing of a water obstacle, physical fitness and hill climbing in the case of a mountain operation, etc., etc.

(b) Sand-table discussions by the Divisional and Brigade Commanders with their subordinate commanders.

(c) A full-scale rehearsal of the operation under conditions approximating as nearly as possible to those of the actual operation.

71. From time to time special conditions of country and enemy tactics will require a new technique to deal with them. The Divisional Commander should make every effort to disengage the necessary formation or unit from battle and, after working out the method to be employed, and holding sand-table discussions, give the troops concerned the opportunity to train on these lines before applying them in action.

72. When a Division is temporarily withdrawn from action the Commander should lay down the type of training which he wishes to take place, leaving it to his subordinate commanders to work out the details.

A good maxim is 'Don't attempt too much'. It is far better to do a little thoroughly than a lot sketchily.

It will pay to concentrate first on the training of officers and NCOs.

Short periods of close drill order should be included in the syllabus for all arms. These will do much to restore quickly any loss of smartness, and pride in personal turn-out and bearing.

Life in the field

The re-enactment photographs in this book were taken by the author courtesy of the East Yorkshire Regiment Living History Group, which re-enacts the exploits of No 10 Platoon, B Company, 2nd Battalion, East Yorkshire Regiment. The unit it remembers, a regular infantry battalion, experienced the highs and lows of war with courage, skill and increasing professionalism. Escaping the fall of France after providing cover to the retreating BEF, it spent four long years training before finally having a chance to return to France. When it did so, it was as one of the first Allied units to set foot on the Normandy beaches. The East Yorkshire Regiment holds a unique position in the history of British troops on D-Day in that two of its battalions – the 2nd and 5th – assaulted in different sectors. The 2nd attacked Sword Beach; the 5th King Red Beach on the westerly Gold Beach. The 2nd Battalion was part of 3rd Infantry Division, Wellington's Iron Division. The East Yorkshire Regiment was fairly typical of the infantry regiments to see action in north-west Europe, and a quick survey of their experiences shows how the story unfolded for many infantry battalions.

I have been helped in this section by the seeing an online copy of Tracy Craggs' PhD dissertation, 'An "Unspectacular" War?', which provides an insightful history of the battalion's progress through north-west Europe.

BELOW Cap badge of the 15th of Foot, the East Yorkshire Regiment. The CO in 1944 was Lt Gen Sir Desmond Anderson.

The 2nd Battalion, East Yorkshire Regiment, 1939–45

Eight East Yorkshire battalions existed during the 1939–45 period:

- **1st Battalion** served in India (1939–42) and Burma.
- **2nd Battalion** fought in France with the BEF, returned to England from the beaches of La Panne near Dunkirk, spent four long years training in England before assaulting on D-Day. It then fought through north-west Europe with British Second Army, capturing Bremen in April 1945. A typical battalion, on D-Day and through north-west Europe, 2/EYorks was part of British 3rd Infantry Division's 8th Infantry Brigade, alongside 1/PWV (the South Lancs Regt) and 1/Suffolk. An infantry battalion in 1944 consisted of a battalion HQ and six companies. Nominal strength was around 845 men armed with rifles (usually SMLE No 4 Mk Is), Sten and Bren guns with supporting weapons – mortars, PIATs and 6pdr anti-tank guns – and carriers (see the table on p. 34).
- **3rd Battalion** unit does not seem to have been raised.
- **4th Battalion**, a TA battalion, fought in France in 1940 and the North African desert as part of 150th Infantry Brigade. It was overrun at the Battle of Gazala in May 1941 and the survivors became PoWs.
- **5th Battalion**, a second-line TA battalion, it fought with 69th Infantry Brigade in Africa, Sicily and north-west Europe, landing on Gold Beach on D-Day.
- **6th Battalion** was a Home Guard battalion.
- **7th Battalion** was disbanded in July 1944, its men serving as replacements in Normandy. At the end of July, Tracy Craggs quotes Lt Col Renison about the large number of replacements from 7th Bn received by the 2nd Battalion: 'magnificent stuff they afterwards proved themselves to be'.
- **8th Battalion** was raised as an AA battalion.

Dating back to 1685, the East Yorks – or 15th Regiment of Foot – had a long history before its postwar amalgamation with the West Yorkshire Regiment (the 14th Foot) in 1958. Its story typifies that of many historied British infantry regiments. Its first major battle was at Killiecrankie in 1689 during the 'Glorious Revolution' that saw William III replace James II as King of England. Its battle honours include: Marlborough's great victories during the War of the Spanish Succession – Blenheim, Ramillies, Oudenarde, Malplaquet – the victories in Canada against the French during the Seven Years' War (Louisbourg, Quebec, 1759), as well as battles in the Caribbean (Martinique, 1762; Havannah, St Lucia, 1778; Martinique, 1794, 1809; Guadeloupe, 1810), the Second Afghan War (Afghanistan, 1879–80) and the Second Boer War (South Africa, 1900–2). Added to that, are most of the major battles of the First World War (when the regiment raised 35 battalions and boasted 21 battle honours) and the Second World War (9 battalions, with one VC earned by Pte Eric Anderson of the 5th Battalion while fighting in Tunisia).

At the outbreak of war the 2nd Battalion was at its camp in Plymouth having recently returned from Palestine. It was mobilised on 7 September 1939. The battalion served in the 8th Infantry Brigade in the 3rd Infantry Division throughout the war, seeing action with the BEF in France in 1939–40 while commanded by the then Maj Gen Bernard Montgomery. 'We are regular soldiers, you and I,' Monty said to the battalion when he visited them, 'and we are going to war with the 3rd Division. I knew it in the last war – it was known as the "Iron Division" then, and it is going to be known as the "Iron Division" in this war. Good luck.'

The 2nd crossed from Southampton to Cherbourg in October 1939. They moved into a position on the Gort Line east of Lille and began an intensive period of training for their part in the Dyle Plan (advancing to the Dyle Canal if the Germans attacked through Belgium). They – along with the rest of the BEF – also rotated to occupy forward positions of the Maginot Line south-east of Luxembourg. The East Yorks went there in January 1940 when they conducted fighting patrols and had their first engagement with the Germans. They returned to the Gort Line to train with the newly arrived men of the Territorial Army.

When the Germans attacked on 9 May, the battalion moved forward as planned, taking up positions to defend Louvain that was probed on the night of 14 May before being vigorously attacked on the 15th. The division held firm, but others to each side did not and soon the BEF was told to withdraw. The 8th Brigade covered that withdrawal. The 3rd Division ended up on the Escaut river with the East Yorks defending Warcoing. Cut off from their lines of communication and running short of ammunition, nevertheless the division held off the Germans when they attacked on the 19th before they were ordered to retreat again back to the Gort Line. After digging in on 23 May, they moved again as the situation deteriorated further, taking up a defensive position at the Yser Canal on 28 May. Here they covered an important sector of the eastern flank of the BEF's route to Dunkirk. They did so and then retreated to the Dunkirk perimeter, fighting off the German advance guard as they did.

The 2nd East Yorks was one of the last battalions to be evacuated during Operation Dynamo, from the beaches of La Panne. It spent 1940–42 on home defence – initially in Sussex and then as part of a mobile reserve – before intense combined operations training saw the battalion earmarked first for the Dieppe raid in 1942 and then the invasion of Sicily. Having been gazumped for both attacks, next they began preparing for the assault on Normandy, exercising in Scotland on the Moray Firth.

It's important here to emphasise the length and depth of their training. Often today we read of problems with the way that the British Army fought in Normandy and that their training was part of the problem. Reading the details of the 2nd Battalion's training gives the lie to this, although it is true that they were not at peak levels all the time in the four years at home. First, physical fitness: from their arrival at Inveraray on 1 May 1942 through to the final days in the 'sausage' camps waiting to embark for Normandy, the East Yorkshires trained physically for the task. On 6 June they were as fit a selection of men as any in any army in Normandy. One of their training marches took them from Inveraray to the Ardnamurchan: a 100-mile march in six days following in the footsteps of their progenitors the 15th Foot, who had trodden similar paths road-making in the aftermath of the Jacobite rebellions. They had exercised day and night, with the intensity rising in 1944:

- 10–11 January: Exercise Grab, three days' training on Sword Beach lookalike Burghead Bay in the Moray Firth
- January/February: street-fighting courses
- February: Exercises Crown and Anchor: 3rd Division exercises
- March: platoon marches
- 15–16 March: Exercise Deputy: training infantry/tank cooperation
- March: Exercise Leapyear: a full-scale rehearsal of the landings
- April: route marches, fitness training
- 3–4 May: Exercise Fabius IV: major rehearsal for the landings took place along the south coast; 2nd Battalion assaulted Littlehampton in stormy conditions. The rehearsal had problems and was not a complete success
- May: beach clearance demonstration by 79th Armoured Division's AVREs
- May: more house and street fighting training
- 26–30 May: detailed briefings take place using models and photographs.

This standard of training may not have been attained by some of the replacements who would fill out 2nd Battalion's ranks as casualties rose. Sometimes coming from different regiments, these men had to be rushed into battle thanks to the high turnover of casualties, particularly junior officers and NCOs, in the fighting. It's also important to remember that training didn't stop once soldiers were in Normandy. During lulls in the fighting, when units were out of the line or before a major operation, much training took place, including combined arms training – infantry with tanks and artillery. Getting to know the people you would fight with helped combined arms operations immensely.

The East Yorkshires underwent a number of changes in the final weeks before D-Day as the older and less capable were winnowed out. The CO, Lt Col Hardy Spicer, was replaced by Lt Col C.F. 'Frank' Hutchinson, and additional men were added to the battalion that had swelled to 1,000 men by the time it assaulted the beaches, the strength including four Canloan officers.

The 8th Brigade was chosen as the assault unit with 185th Brigade following up and 9th in

ABOVE Wearing a camouflaged windproof smock, turtle (Mk III) helmet and carrying his SMLE with pigsticker bayonet attached, our reenactor represents a late war infantryman (compare with photo on p. 91). Note the complete lack of badges and insignia.

reserve. They embarked by Saturday 3 June and waited in Portsmouth Harbour for the off.

Between 04:30 and 06:00 on D-Day, the assault landing craft were lowered from the Empire *Battleaxe* and HMS *Glenearn* to start the seven-mile journey to the beaches. In his LCA Maj Charles K. 'Banger' King regaled the men of HQ Platoon, A Company with lines from Shakespeare's *King Henry V*. At 07:25 the East Yorks landed on Sword's Queen Red beach where heavy mortar, machine gun and artillery fire were encountered.

A and B Companies, supported by the tanks of 13th/18th Hussars and AVREs of 5th Assault Regt, RE, were to break through the beach obstacles. Then A Company, along with C Company of 1/South Lancs, would attack and eliminate Strongpoint Cod (the Germans dubbed it StP20 La Brèche). Defended by German 10./Grenadier Regiment 736 this consisted of a 75mm Pak40, two 50mm anti-tank guns, three mortars, a 37mm gun and four Tobruk machine-gun posts. Then they would move on to Strongpoints Sole and Daimler.

In fact the tanks were slow to arrive, and the attack was undertaken by the infantry alone. By 08:30 8th Brigade had cleared the beach and Strongpoint Cod was taken by 10:00. B Company moved inland – over a flooded marshy area – and assaulted Strongpoint Sole with C Company in support. StP14 Ouistreham – with an R634 six-embrasure turret, a 50mm anti-tank gun, two mortars, a 20mm Flak 30 and three Tobruks – was overrun by 13:00

with assistance from the SP guns of 76th Field Regt, RA. This support was necessary because the tanks hadn't kept up and the naval FOO had been killed.

The next task was to attack and eliminate Daimler Battery – WN12 Ouistreham Château d'eau – a battery of four 155mm howitzers (4./Artillery-Regiment 1716) capable of firing on to the invasion beaches, with local protection of three Tobruks and two 20mm Flak 30s. This was the main responsibility of A and C Companies, supported by tanks of the 13th/18th Hussars who laid smoke as the attack went in. Daimler Battery was put out of action by 18:00 with 70 prisoners in the bag.

The East Yorks continued on to the village of St-Aubin-d'Arquenay where they were relieved by the King's Own Scottish Borderers. The East Yorks spent the night in a cornfield near Hermanville. The War Diary identifies the 6 June casualties numbering 209: 5 officers and 60 men killed, and 4 officers and 140 men wounded or missing – a quarter of their nominal strength. On the 7th the regiment received 3 officers and 60 ORs as reinforcements.

Tracy Craggs discusses in some detail the allegation – almost certainly specious but promoted by Brigadier The Lord Lovat in his autobiography – that the 8th Brigade didn't perform well, 'A poor showing in the last rehearsal was faithfully repeated on the battlefield. We passed through them, leaving platoons scrabbling in sand where the shelling hit hardest.' Another baleful account

RIGHT The beach the 2nd Battalion landed on – Queen Red sector, Sword Beach – was well defended. The wire defences seen here would have had minefields behind and the Beach Group would have been involved in clearing these. This photograph shows both commandos of 1st Special Service Brigade, some with bicycles, and vehicles of the East Yorks (Universal Carrier with number 56).

was in Cornelius Ryan's *The Longest Day*, which – apart from getting the unit number wrong – quoted a commando as saying he was 'aghast to see the East Yorks lying in bunches . . . it would probably never have happened had they spread out' – missing the fact that the commandos, too, were sustaining casualties. Of Philippe Kieffer's 177 men of 1st BFM French Commando landing with No 4 Cdo, 21 were killed and 93 wounded; No 4 Cdo itself lost 45 dead and 212 wounded. However you look at it, the East Yorks sustained the highest casualties of the 8th Brigade's landings (the South Lancs lost 49 dead, 89 wounded and 19 missing; 1/Suffolk 12 dead, 25 wounded and 4 missing). Among the casualties were the MO ('hit on disembarking'), D Company commander ('when a mortar bomb burst among the Coy HQ') and the battalion CO, Frank Hutchinson, who was replaced by Lt Col N.J. Dickson). Queen Red Beach was not a good place to be on 6 June: 3rd Division as a whole suffered 718 dead and 5,216 wounded/missing – 21% of its attacking force of 25,929.

The battalion's next major battle was another stiff fight – on 27–28 June during Operation Epsom, remembered for the fighting around the Château de la Londe, dubbed the 'bloodiest square mile in the whole of Normandy'. In Operation Mitten 8th Brigade assaulted the area, which was heavily defended, and then withstood a counter-attack supported by armour. The East Yorks' butcher's bill, as noted in the War Diary, was 111 killed, wounded or missing – helping bring the total for other ranks and officers for June to 382 (although, as the diary notes, many of the missing were accounted for later):

	Offrs	ORs
Killed	7	83
Wounded	13	266
Missing	0	13
Total	20	362

Putting this into perspective, a rifle company had about 5 officers and 124 men. The 2nd Battalion landed on D-Day overstrength (around 880 men). Within a month at least a third of their number were casualties.

The East Yorks fought on through Normandy receiving reinforcements from the disbanded 7th Battalion and, later, from the disbanded 59th Division at the end of August when the 2nd East Yorks was, briefly, overstrength. Fighting on into Belgium, the East Yorks fought their way across the Escaut Canal and protected XXX Corps' right flank during Operation Market Garden. Its next bout of heavy fighting came in October during Operation Aintree on the Maas – some of the hardest fighting since Normandy – at Overloon and Venray. After the fighting, men of the regiment received their first leave since D-Day. They needed it: 3rd Division's monthly medical bulletins showed that during the battle, for every two battle casualties there was one exhaustion case. Much of this was put down to the awful weather conditions and long periods at the front under shellfire. On 19 October, battalion CO Lt Col N.J. Dickson left because of ill health and 2IC Lt Col J.D.W. Renison took over.

The next big operation was the First Canadian Army's Operation Veritable, starting on 8 February. Hampered by weather and German flooding that stopped the American southern attack (Operation Grenade), the Canadians made slow progress through the well-defended Reichswald. The 3rd Division was involved after these battles, attacking from Goch as part of Operation Blockbuster that kick-started the advance now that the Americans were finally able to cross the River Roer. The 2/EYorks' part was Operation Heather: taking a bridge over the Mühlen-Fleuth stream – the Schaddenhof bridge that would be dubbed Yorkshire bridge after the battle. With help from corps artillery, the battalion fulfilled its mission and fought off the determined German Fallschirmjäger counter-attacks. Afterwards, 83 enemy dead were counted and 150 PoWs were taken; 2/EYorks had suffered 156 casualties.

ABOVE Men of 2/EYorks under fire during an advance near Caen. The Yorkshire rose on the sergeant's left arm identifies the unit. Note the 'turtle' helmets. They used the same liners as the Brodie Mk II helmet and replaced the earlier type during 1944.

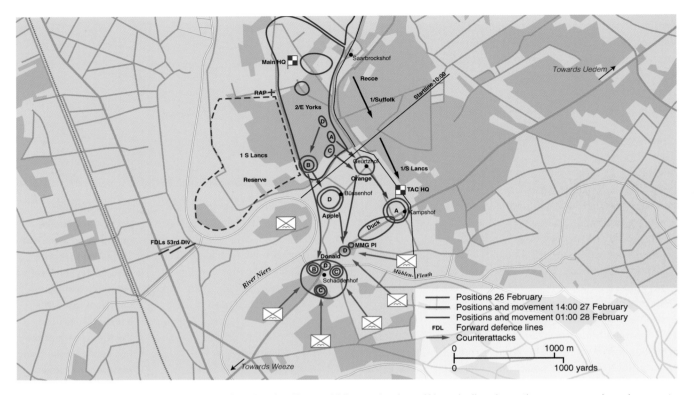

Positions 26 February
Positions and movement 14:00 27 February
Positions and movement 01:00 28 February
FDL Forward defence lines
→ Counterattacks

0   1000 m
0   1000 yards

ABOVE The battle for what became known as Yorkshire Bridge.

At the height of the battle, 'Banger' King arrived with a carrier full of ammunition for C Company, having driven through enemy lines. He was awarded the bar to his DSO for his valour. On 2 and 3 March 1945 the battalion received a draft of 172 reinforcements.

The battalion didn't take part in the Rhine Crossing but returned to the front line in mid-April, still engaging in small, bitter battles with house-to-house fighting. During one of these actions 'Banger' King was killed and the whole battalion mourned. The attack on Bremen was the last action of the campaign for the 2nd Battalion. The Battalion spent VE Day in Westphalia where they were employed as part of the army of occupation.

The men of the re-enactment society remember, as should we all, the sacrifices of the men of the East Yorks fighting for their country and freedom. From landing in Normandy to the end of the war 2/East Yorks had 1,072 casualties – not the most: 4/Somerset LI had 1,313 and others more. The official strength of an infantry battalion in 1944–45 was 845 officers and men; 1,072 casualties is the equivalent of 8½ rifle companies. The press

CONTINUED ON PAGE 79

RIGHT AND FAR RIGHT The men in the 'now' version of this photograph are from the 1st Battalion, 1st Royal Norfolk Regiment of 185th Infantry Brigade, 3rd Division, and are seen on 26 November in the Netherlands. They wear the same mix of clothing and carry the same weapons that the 2nd Battalion would have had.

LIFE IN THE FIELD

It's impossible today to portray accurately the life of an infantryman during wartime. Books and films can try, but the constant sense of threat, danger and loss of life are impossible to replicate. The photos in this section give a taste of some of the out-of-action elements.

ABOVE These British troops are dug in on the edge of a field overlooking Hill 112 in the Odon Valley – scene of heavy fighting between 43rd (Wessex) Division and II SS-Panzer Corps (9th SS-Pz Div Hohenstaufen, 10th SS-Pz Div Frundsberg and the Tiger Is of Schwere SS-Pz-Bn 102) in July 1944. While his mate keeps watch, an exhausted infantry sleeps in his slit trench.

BELOW South Saskatchewan soldiers relax on 8 August 1944, after capturing Rocquancourt the previous night. L/Cpl Krushelinski bathes his feet while Pte Balogh (centre) and L/Cpl Kostyk enjoy a Pernod (if the bottle on the table is accurately labelled!).

ABOVE Water, obviously, is at a premium in the desert – making an impromptu bath even more sweet.

ABOVE RIGHT Discipline and morale go hand in hand – and Slim was able to turn round the British defeats in Burma through training and discipline. Here, as one man writes a letter home, his tattooed mate shaves. Weapons litter the area: a Sten and a 2in mortar as well as two Lee-Enfields.

BELOW The importance of post to and from the front cannot be over-emphasised. This field service postcard (Army Form A 2042) may have been brief but it reached the recipient quickly (12 hours quoted from north-west Europe) and was free to use. The information in this one would have been happily received (although it was sent before the major fighting in France started):

I am quite well
I have received your letter
  dated 15-3-40
Parcel dated 15-3-40
Letter follows at first
  opportunity
Bob
24-3-40
(RCT)

LEFT Men of 9th Cameronians (15th (Scottish) Division) attend a service led by Rev S. Cook just behind the front line during the afternoon of 25 June 1944. These men were to go into battle for the first time on the following day, which may account for the singing gusto. The Museum of Army Chaplaincy notes that 96 British and 38 Commonwealth chaplains died during the war and that many carried out the ministries in more than difficult circumstances: 30 were captured at Dunkirk; others took part in the building of the Burma Railway, Changi prison and the hell of Shamshuipo PoW camp during the 1942 diphtheria epidemic.

BELOW All armies tried to bolster their front-line troops' morale with entertainments and concert parties. The Americans had the United States Organizations' Camp Shows; the British ENSA (sometimes remembered as 'Every Night Something Awful'); while the Canadians had The Army Show. This Canadian 'Invasion Revue' took place at Banville on 30 July 1944 near the Advanced Landing Ground (ALG) B-3 Sainte-Croix-sur-Mer. It's worth noting that 20 miles to the south-west, Operation Bluecoat started that same day, showing how much change there could be within short distances in Normandy at the time. *(via PhotosNormandie)*

Jungle rations

Supply was often difficult in the jungle and air-supply became a regular occurrence. The British developed Jungle Ration Mk 1 in 1942, criticisms of which led to Jungle Ration Mk II. This supplied a day's ration for two men. Contents were:

- 1 tin (5oz or 7oz) of one of four flavours: (1) Fish and egg, (2) Breakfast pork, (3) Ham and egg, or (4) Chopped liver and bacon (the breakfast meat portion)
- 1 tin (10–14oz) of one of four flavours: (1) Preserved meat (Bully beef), (2) Meat and kidney pudding, (3) Stewed steak (or Irish stew), (4) Chopped ham and beef
- 1 square metal tin, containing: Oatmeal blocks (two single cubes or a double stick, generally made in Canada); Biscuits plain and/or enriched chocolate (high temperature, various flavours); Milk powder (boxed) or Sweetened condensed milk (foil tube); Tea blocks (tea, sugar and whitener combo sufficient for one 12oz mug each) OR Tea tablets (very strong compressed tea in a small drum called SBC 'Service Blend, Compressed') OR Tea bags (Canadian Red Rose); Salt tablets; Vitamin tablets (chewable flavoured ones); Boiled sweets; Jam (pressed); Cheese (tin or foil tube); Sugar tablets (eight of

them); Salt (boxed); Chewing gum; Fizz tablets (vitamin enriched); Lemon crystals; Matches; Latrine paper
- Tin of 20 cigarettes.

(Source: http://17thdivision.tripod.com/index.html)

All component portions of the ration were lacquered/painted in a green colour, with the notable exception of the pressed jam (which came in a clear cellophane wrapper), the chewing gum, matches and the latrine paper. The sizes and manufacturers of the tinned goods, as well as the crackers and overall outer tin size, changed throughout the Mk II rations' lifespan.

ABOVE The Americans would call it a 'chow line', the Canadian caption mentions 'dinner parade'. Food is served to men of the Highland Light Infantry of Canada in Thaon, 6 August 1944. *(Lt Ken Bell/Library and Archives Canada PA-132829)*

RATION CONTENTS (Facsimiles of content listings and suggested use)

MESS TIN RATION

SCALE:—

Biscuits, service	9 ozs.	In 1 sealed tin which fits in the larger half of the mess tin.		All tins, including Tommy cookers and also the matches are delivered to the ships in bulk quantities, e.g. cheese tins in boxes of one gross 1.5oz tins and marked S.R.D. ♣ CHEESE.
Biscuits, sweet	3 ozs.			
Raisin chocolate	8 ozs.			
Sweets, boiled	4½ ozs.			
Cheese (2 × 1.5 oz. tins)	3 ozs.	These tins fit in second half of mess tin.		
Dipping spread (1 tin)	2 ozs.			
Tea, sugar, milk powder (1 tin)	5 ozs.			
Meat, preserved	12 ozs.			
Miniature safety matches	1 box			

1 Tommy cooker (round type) to be carried separately.
NOTE. The tea, sugar, milk powder produces 5–6 pints of tea.

Designed to give a man enough energy for 24 hours – important during assaults or in action – this British ration included compressed blocks of meat and oatmeal both of which needed to be broken down in hot water to be palatable.

INSTRUCTIONS for the use of "THE 24-HOUR RATION"

1. CONTENTS.

This box contains the full rations (in concentrated form) for one man for one day as follows:—

10 biscuits.

2 sweetened oatmeal blocks.

  tea/sugar/milk blocks (May be wrapped together).

1 meat block (May be several wrapped together).

2 slabs of raisin chocolate.

1 slab of plain chocolate.

boiled sweets.

2 packets of chewing gum.

1 packet of salt.

meat extract tablet(s).

4 tablets of sugar.

Latrine paper 4 pieces.

2. SUGGESTED MENU.

Breakfast

2 oatmeal porridge blocks.

2 biscuits.

tea blocks (one half of quantity provided).

After breakfast remove 2 or 3 biscuits, chocolate, chewing gum and sweets and place in convenient pockets for use during action, thus being more readily available when required.

Supper

Meat block(s).

Biscuits.

Tea blocks (one half of quantity provided).

Any sweets, chocolate etc., left over from the day.

Please turn over.

3. PREPARATION.

To prepare a hot meal, crumble the blocks up finely into a mess tin. Add water to a depth of about ½" (½ pint) for the 2 oatmeal blocks and the meat block(s), and about 1" (1 pint) for half the quantity of tea blocks provided. Boil with stirring for 3–4 minutes. If circumstances make heating water impossible, the oatmeal and meat blocks can be eaten dry – in which case

    (1) Eat them slowly.

    (2) Chew them well.

    (3) Drink some water at the same time or soon after.

4. NOTES.

(a) The amount of water suggested is only approximate.

(b) Cook the meat and porridge (oatmeal) carefully or they will burn.

(c) Broken biscuits and meat extract tablets may be added to the meat stew if required.

(d) After boiling, leave the tea for a few minutes so that the leaves can sink to the bottom of the mess-tin. Add sugar if required.

(e) If you want more hot drink, cook up the broken bar of plain chocolate with water or dissolve the meat extract tablets in hot water.

(f) It is more economical for men to cook in pairs and make the larger part of the mess tin full of tea to give nearly two pints (using all tea blocks in one pack). It is essential to use cookers away from all draughts – using a tin as a shield or by making a small slit trench.

Please turn over.

(14 men for one day.)
Contents and suggested use.

BREAKFAST.

Tea*	3 tins (2 tall, 1 flat – Tea, Sugar and Milk Mixture).
+ Sausage (1 hour)	2 tins.
Biscuit*	1 tin.
Margarine*	1 tin.

(*Items marked thus are also to provide for other meals.)

DINNER.

+ Steak and kidney pudding (½ hour)	11 tins.
+ Vegetables (¾ hour)	4 tins (2 large, 2 small).
Tinned fruits	2 tins.

TEA.

Tea	– (* see above.)
Biscuit	– (* see above.)
Margarine	– (* see above.)
Jam	1 tin.

SUPPER.

+ Baked beans (¾ hour)	3 tins.
Biscuit	– (* see above.)

EXTRAS.

Cigarettes	2 tins (1 round, 1 flat – 7 cigarettes for each man).
Sweets	1 tin.
Salt	– (packed with sweets above.)
Matches	– (packed with sweets above.)
Chocolate	– (1 slab for each man – packed with biscuit.)
Latrine paper.	

Directions.

Tea, sugar and milk powder. Use a dry spoon and sprinkle powder on heated water and bring to the boil, stirring well. Three heaped teaspoonfuls to 1 pint of water.

+ May be eaten hot or cold. To heat, place unopened tins in boiling water for minimum period as indicated. Sausage may be fried (using margarine) if preferred.

++ This is only one of nine types. The others are B, C, D, E, F, G and X and Y, containing items such as:—

Type.	Breakfast.	Dinner.	Tea/Supper.		
B	Bacon	Steak and kidney	Jam	Date pudding	Soup
C	Sausage	Irish stew	Cheese	Sultana pudding	Soup
D	Bacon	Stewed steak	Sardines	Rice pudding	Soup
E	Sausage	Haricot oxtail	Sardines	Marmalade pudding	Cheese
F	Luncheon meat	Preserved meat	Jam		
	Mixed fruit pudding	Salmon			
		Soup			
G	Sausage	M and V ration	Jam	Treacle pudding	Soup
X	Luncheon meat	Preserved meat	Jam		
	Tinned fruit	Salmon			
		Soup			
Y	Sausage	M and V ration	Sardines	Tinned fruit	Soup

(Source: https://www.oldtimedesigncompany.co.uk/24-hour-rations)

ABOVE Another morale booster: a Christmas meal in the jungle. There are many stories of Christmas goodies dropped by air to the men of Fourteenth Army and their supporting arms.

Demob

'The only time I voted Labour.' My Conservative father-in-law was not the only member of the armed forces who voted Churchill out because he felt the Labour demobilisation plan would get him home more quickly. As it happened, it didn't. A useful major, the age-and-service scheme kept him in the field for some time in spite of serving through the war. First to go were men over 50 and married women (if they wanted to). Slow demobilisation led to frustration and friction, and even mutiny.

The plans for demobilisation had been discussed by the government since early 1944 and were detailed in September that year. It still took over two years to get most of the 5 million servicemen and women back on to 'Civvy Street'. The servicemen arriving back in the UK first went to a Military Disembarkation Camp where, they were advised, they would stay for 12–18 hours depending on train departure timings. There they would be expected to hand back all except their clothing and personal kit. They then went to the Military Dispersal Unit they had chosen. *Hansard* supplies a list of these centres, reproduced in the accompanying table:

Military Disembarkation Camp (MDC) Units		
Command or District	*Title of Unit*	*Location*
Southern	No 1 MDC Unit	Ranikhet Camp, Reading
	No 2 MDC, Unit	Slade Camp, Oxford
Eastern	No 3 MDC Unit	Moore Barracks, Shorncliffe, Kent
Western	No 1 MDC,Group HQ	Hadrian's Camp, Carlisle
	No 4 MDC Unit	Ditto
	No 5 MDC Unit	Ditto
Northern	No 6 MDC Unit	Queen Elizabeth Barracks, Strensall, York

Military Dispersal Units (MDU)		
Command or District	*Title of Unit*	*Location*
Scottish	No1 MDU	Redford Barracks, Edinburgh
Northern	No 2 MDU	Fulford Barracks, York
Eastern	No 3 MDU	Talavera Camp, Northampton
	No 5 MDU	Queen's Camp, Guildford
London	No 4 MDU	Regent's Park Barracks, Albany St, NW1
Southern	No 6 MDU	Sherford Camp, Taunton
Western	No 7 MDU	North and South Camps, Ashton-under-Lyne
	No 8 MDU	Bradbury Lines, Hereford
Northern Ireland	No 9 Combined Military	Victoria Barracks, Belfast
	Collecting and Dispersal Unit	

At the MDU they received:

- documentation (unemployment book, health insurance book, temporary ration card – they received permanent ration books, clothing coupons and an ID card once they got home)
- a grant (three weeks' pay)
- a demob suit – hat, three-piece suit or trousers and jacket, two shirts, a tie, a raincoat and a pair of shoes. Of course, not everything fitted well and the demob suit went down in history as the inspiration of many a stand-up comedian's routine
- cigarettes, clothing coupons and a rail pass home.

Once the returning men and women reached home – and in many places such as London's East End they returned to devastation – they had to contend with a very different set of pressures to those they had faced in service. It is not a surprise to learn of rising divorce rates in the later 1940s. Rationing also came as a shock and continued into the 1950s.

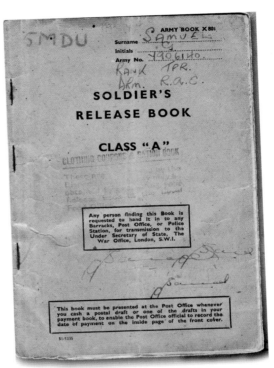

LEFT All good things come to an end! This page of Army Book X 801 identifies the Release Leave to which a trooper in the Sharpshooters was entitled: he left on 12 February 1946 and was paid until 9 April unless he was transferred to the Reserve, upon which he would receive Reserve pay. (RCT)

Chapter Four

Uniform and equipment

━━━━━━━⬤━━━━━━━

Central to the infantryman's equipment was the introduction of the Pattern 1937 Webbing, a development of the 1908 pattern but lighter in weight – 'designed to meet modern conditions of warfare ... it is easy to assemble and adjust; and possesses the important feature that no articles are suspended below the waistline (except the bayonet and the officer's haversack) to impede the wearer. ... Waterproofed and dyed in the yarn ... the fabric [is] practically impervious to the weather'.

OPPOSITE A late war scene in Flushing (Vlissingen) in November 1944 during Operation Infatuate I. Landings by No 4 Commando were followed up by 156th (Scottish) Infantry Brigade attached to First Canadian Army. Armed with Sten guns and Lee-Enfields, the men wear windproof smocks and camouflage scrim scarves. The windproof smock and trousers were issued in the winter of 1944.

| Field Marshal | General | Lieutenant General | Major General | Brigadier | Colonel | Lieutenant Colonel | Major | Captain | Lieutenant | Second Lieutenant |

Officer shoulder badges used in the British, Dominion and Commonwealth armies. *(RCT/Eleanor Forty)*

Rank and insignia

British ranks*

Rank (Abbreviation)	Symbol/Badge	Notes
Officers		
Field Marshal (FM)	Crown above crossed batons surrounded by a wreath	The baton was a symbol of the rank. There were only eight British FMs in the Second World War (Alexander, Brooke, Dill, Gort, Ironside, Montgomery, Wavell, Wilson)
General (Gen)	Crown above a star above crossed sabre and baton	Army commander
Lieutenant General (Lt Gen)	Crown above crossed sabre and baton	Corps commander
Major General (Maj Gen)	A star above crossed sabre and baton	Division commander
Brigadier (Brig)	Crown above three stars (one above the other two)	Brigade commander
Colonel (Col**)	Crown above two stars (one above the other)	Administrative position; not a field command
Lieutenant Colonel (Lt Col)	Crown above a star	CO of a battalion or regiment
Major (Maj)	Crown	2IC of a battalion or regiment; OC of a company
Captain (Capt)	Three stars in line	2IC of a company
Lieutenant (Lt)	Two stars in line	Commander of a platoon
Second Lieutenant (2Lt)	A star	Commander of a platoon
Other ranks – Non-commissioned officers		
Warrant Officer Class I (WOI)	Royal Arms on the lower arm	Various appointments. In a regiment would be RSM
Warrant Officer Class II (WOII)	Laurel wreath on the lower arm	CSM or RQSM
Warrant Officer Class III (WOIII)	Crown on lower sleeve.	Rank discontinued in 1941. Platoon sergeant major commanding a platoon. When discontinued, many WOIIIs were commissioned
Staff Sergeant (S/Sgt)	A crown above three chevrons	CQMS.
Sergeant (Sgt)	Three chevrons	Often platoon 2IC and usually the most experienced man in the unit
Corporal (Cpl)	Two chevrons	Often a section leader
Lance Corporal (L/Cpl)	Single chevron on both arms	
Private (Pte), Guardsman, Fusilier, Rifleman	No badge of rank	The lowest rank in the army; could wear proficiency badges

NCO badges of rank were worn on the arm.

(Sodacan/WikiCommons CC BY-SA 4.0)

| Lance Corporal | Corporal | Sergeant | Staff Sergeant | WO III | WO II | WO I |

Notes: * Temporary/acting ranks were sometimes necessary because of wartime exigencies. During the war there were a number of types of officers' rank:

Brevet: Discontinued during the war, brevet ranks (usually captains to colonel) had rank privileges (seniority on the Army list, rank badge etc) but not the pay and allowances of the rank.

Acting: Officers promoted to an Acting rank had to relinquish the rank if no other similar appointment could be found. However, after three months or longer (time varied depending on rank) the rank would automatically become a Temporary rank. Didn't carry the pay and allowances of the rank.

Temporary: Given for a unpredetermined period of time, the officer reverted to his Substantive rank or War Substantive rank. Didn't carry the pay and allowances of the rank.

Substantive: A confirmed rank that can only be taken away by a court martial.

War Substantive: Given during the period of the hostilities through to 1946–47. If promoted to a Temporary rank two grades above his Substantive/War Substantive rank, the officer would be promoted automatically to the War Substantive rank below the Temporary rank. So, a Substantive Captain promoted Temporary Colonel would also be promoted to War Substantive Lieutenant Colonel. Didn't carry the pay and allowances of the rank.

Local: Granted for a specific geographical area.

**** Colonels are not field commanders. It was a staff posting. Note also that the Colonel-in-Chief of a regiment is usually a member of the royal family and that a colonel of a regiment is often a general: it's an honorary position.

Badges and insignia

The British Army, as with all the major combatants, spent a great deal of time and effort ensuring that the armed forces had the uniforms and equipment they needed. Their success is debatable: look no further than the imbalance between British and German armour. This was not only a tactical issue. British armour – in particular tank guns – didn't really reach parity until the Firefly. In order to ensure the army had anti-tank guns the 2pdr was continued in production when it was obsolescent. The mainstay of the Royal Artillery, the 25pdr, took well over two years to reach significant availability. Appeasement, naval and air force requirements and the debacle in France in 1940 didn't help, but the wise heads in the War Office

BELOW An outstanding corps commander, this study of Lt Gen Guy Simonds shows him in Italy when he was GOC 5th Canadian Armoured Division. Previously, he had commanded 1st Infantry Division and he would leave Italy in January 1944 to command II Canadian Corps. Note his general's cap and shoulder badges, collar gorget, Canada shoulder flash and the maroon rectangle that identified 5th Division (also on his jeep's pennant). The bonnet of the jeep has an RAF roundel to minimise the risk from friendly aircraft. *(Library and Archives Canada)*

RIGHT Colour backings
for officers' cloth
rank badges were:
red – staff (colonels
and upward who didn't
wear the uniform of
a specific regiment
or corps), RA, RAOC,
Pioneer Corps and
CMP; yellow – RAC,
RASC and RAPC; blue
– RE and RSigs; scarlet
– infantry (other than
Rifles) and general list;
Rifle green – infantry
(Rifles); Cambridge
blue – AAC and AEC;
purple – RAChD;
dull cherry – RAMC;
dark blue – REME;
green – AD Corps and
Intelligence Corps; grey
– ACC; black – APTC.

didn't cover themselves with glory when it came to defence procurement. Questions were asked in the House!

That being said, it's hard to fault the War Office when it comes to uniform or infantry weapons. They may not have had the dark magnetism of the parade-ground German Army and SS uniforms, but British infantry

BELOW Taken on 15 June 1944 in Hérouvillette (south of Ranville), this photograph shows three men from D Company, 2nd Oxford and Buckinghamshire Light Infantry who took part in the daring coup de main attack on the bridges over the Caen Canal and River Orne. They are (left to right): Pte Frank Gardener, Capt Brian Priday (the company 2IC who landed near Varaville) and L/Cpl Lambley. They are wearing Denison smocks and para helmets. Note Lambley's single chevron (denoting his rank of lance corporal).

clothing and equipment was much better than some postwar commentators would have you believe. The same was true for their weapons: the PIAT looked like a Heath-Robinson machine but it killed 7% of German armour in Normandy and its lack of backblast didn't give away its position every time it fired. The Bren gun may not have been able to match the 'Spandau' for its suppressive rate of fire, but it was more accurate, could be easily carried, used by one man and didn't have trailing belts to get caught in vegetation. British battledress may have been prone to wrinkling around the elbow and wasn't the smartest on the parade ground, but it was designed for combat – for comfort rather than cut. With the various climates and needs of an empire that stretched across the globe, British uniforms were tailored to their use and their environment and were copied by American and German forces.

The British Army was mechanised: battledress was designed to have nothing that could catch, purpose-built to fit the webbing that was capable of carrying everything needed by a soldier in combat, unlike the Germans, who, veterans say, announced their presence from afar as their many bags and packs rattled together. The cut of battledress was to help drivers or riflemen lying prone – not Hugo Boss-clad parade popinjays.

However, as with all armies, there was one area that complicated the ergonomic battledress: the idiosyncratic accoutrements that adorned it. A range of headgear – berets, peaked caps, service caps, bonnets, Glengarrys, Solar pith hats, slouch hats, cap comforters – and then the badges, armlets, shoulder straps, lanyards and other means of identification that were attached to shoulders, arms and breasts. Rank, trades, proficiency at arms, arms of service, regimental and other formation identification, wound stripes and service chevrons: there were insignia for everything and they were worn with pride. It's difficult to wean soldiers away from their insignia.

Badges

Many metal and cloth badges were worn by officers and ORs, from cap badges, shoulder flashes, rank badges, regimental badges, through to badges for trades (usually worn on right sleeve), instructors (worn on both

ABOVE Lt Gen Brian Horrocks, commander of XXX Corps was one of Montgomery's most trusted and reliable generals. Note his general's cap badge and corps shoulder insignia.

ABOVE The 'Paschal Lamb' cap badge and 'Queens' shoulder flash show these men to be part of the Queen's Royal Regiment (West Surrey), second only in precedence as infantry of the line to the 1st of Foot, the Royal Scots. Originally part of 44th (Home Counties) Infantry Division, with whom they served as part of the BEF in 1940, on 1 November they became part of 131st Lorried Infantry Brigade, 7th Armoured Division (accounting for the Desert Rat badge). They served with the Desert Rats for the rest of the war.

BELOW There were a number of qualification badges, mainly worn on the lower arm as here with this qualified signaller (note crossed flags) from D/Régiment de Maisonneuve. He's talking on a No 18 wireless set outside Cuyk, Netherlands, on 23 January 1945. *(Lt Michael M. Dean/Library and Archives Canada PA-190099)*

ABOVE Similar badges – Royal Signals infantry operator wireless operator badge (top) and RAOC wireless technician's skill at arms badge (above).

BELOW Army Operator Wireless and Keyboard Badge. There were many different tradesmen's and instructors' badges, as well as the skill at arms badges. They were all important because having them ensured more pay. *(Badges: RPJ Militaria)*

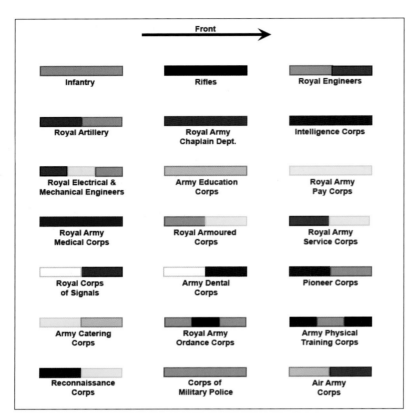

Front →

Infantry	Rifles	Royal Engineers
Royal Artillery	Royal Army Chaplain Dept.	Intelligence Corps
Royal Electrical & Mechanical Engineers	Army Education Corps	Royal Army Pay Corps
Royal Army Medical Corps	Royal Armoured Corps	Royal Army Service Corps
Royal Corps of Signals	Army Dental Corps	Pioneer Corps
Army Catering Corps	Royal Army Ordance Corps	Army Physical Training Corps
Reconnaissance Corps	Corps of Military Police	Air Army Corps

ABOVE The arm of service strips (2in long by 0.25in deep) were worn on each BD sleeve just below any formation badge.

POLAND
AIRBORNE
K.O.S.B.
ESSEX
SEAFORTH CANADA

ABOVE Cloth shoulder insignia.

RIGHT This jacket has the badges of Eighth Army and the Royal Signals shoulder and arm of service – blue and white, with the blue forward.
(Royal Signals Museum)

sleeves) and skill at arms (issued 1936–43 as a result of competitions, the winners wearing the badge on the left forearm). Most were worn on battledress, some on greatcoats. For more details see Brian L. Davis's *British Army Uniforms & Insignia of World War Two*. Examples are:

Hammer & pincers	Armament artificers, armourers, fitters and smiths
Crossed hatchets	Pioneers (grenade over = Fusilier regiments; bugle over = Light Infantry or Rifle regiments)
Crossed rifles	Musketry instructor
Crossed swords	PT instructors
Crossed flags	Signalling instructors

Arm of service colours

ACI (Army Council Instruction) 1118 of 1940 laid down that to distinguish between services of the army, an arm of service strip was to be worn by all ranks on battledress and the greatcoat.

Army Air Corps	Cambridge blue and blue
Army Catering Corps	Grey and yellow
Army Educational Corps	Cambridge blue
Army Physical Training Corps	Black, red, black
Corps of Military Police	Red
Corps of Royal Electrical and Mechanical Engineers	Red, yellow, blue
Infantry regiments	Scarlet
Infantry Rifle regiments	Rifle green
Intelligence Corps	Green
Pioneer Corps	Red and green
Reconnaissance Corps	Yellow and green
Royal Armoured Corps	Yellow forward and red
Royal Army Chaplains' Department	Purple
Royal Army Dental Corps	Green and white
Royal Army Medical Corps	Dull cherry red
Royal Army Ordnance Corps	Red, blue, red
Royal Army Pay Corps	Yellow
Royal Army Service Corps	Yellow and blue
Royal Artillery	Red and blue
Royal Engineers	Blue and red
Royal Corps of Signals	Blue and white
Staff	Red

LEFT The medals of Captain E.G. Harrison, Royal Signals. Left to right: OBE, MC, BEM, 1939–45 Star, Africa Star, Italy Star, France and Germany Star, Defence and War Medals. Nine stars were issued for the campaigns of the Second World War. The ribbon colours have symbolic significance (it is said that they were designed by King George VI himself). The colours of the France and Germany Star's ribbon (blue/white/red/white/blue) represent the national colours of the United Kingdom, France and the Netherlands.
(Royal Signals Museum)

Decorations

British medals, gallantry awards, decorations and orders provide a subject in themselves and are well covered in many books.

- Gallantry awards – such as the Victoria Cross, Military Cross and Military Medal, Distinguished Service Order and Medal – were awarded to individuals for a conspicuous act of valour, usually in the presence of the enemy, while serving in the British, Dominion and Commonwealth armed forces.
- Campaign medals and clasps were awarded after the war for service. The land-based are, in order they should be worn: 1939–45 Star, Africa Star, Pacific Star (clasp Burma), Burma star (clasp Pacific), Italy Star, France and Germany Star, Defence Medal, Canadian Volunteer Service Medal, War Medal 1939–45.
- Service medals – given for long and distinguished service.

Uniforms

Before the advent of accurate long-range armaments and aircraft, troops were dressed in some form of distinctive uniform along with identifying badges, crests and so on, in order to be very obviously seen and recognised both on and off the battlefield. Initially a single uniform covered all eventualities and troops fought in the same ceremonial kit that they paraded in. This martial display was usually peacock-bright and shiny, but as gunpowder weapons improved by the mid-19th century, marksmen and snipers began wearing more inconspicuous clothing to conceal themselves while hunting targets.

While in India the British military khaki evolved from soldiers dyeing their white uniforms to reduce their visibility from a distance. However, it was not until the 20th century that any serious effort was made to replace parade-style uniforms with clothing simpler for wear in actual combat. By the First World War a more camouflaged approach was taken to prevent soldiers being such obvious targets for the increasing accuracy and lethality of modern weaponry. For the British the nondescript khaki became the chosen colour and combat uniforms were produced that were much more simple and robust, as were all the various items of personal equipment that were now issued to every soldier. Parade uniforms still existed but were no longer worn in battle, being kept instead for ceremonial purposes.

The rules covering army dress were identified for commissioned officers in *Dress Regulations for the Army* (Dress Regulations). Published in June 1934, the regulations were amended in 1937, 1938 and 1940. The rules

LEFT Capt Harrison served, as did many, in North Africa, Italy, France and Germany. There were various other land-based theatre stars. This is the one allocated to those who fought in Burma. Others include the Atlantic, Pacific and Arctic stars. Note that the stars were issued unnamed.
(Royal Signals Museum)

RIGHT AND BELOW
Officer's 1937 webbing: compass pouch and binoculars case, water bottle and map case, ammo pouch, pistol holster and haversack. The 1937 webbing was designed to accommodate all soldiers from all arms. Note the officer's haversack (bottom left), a rectangular bag 12in (wide) × 9in (high) × 2in (deep). It was designed to carry pencils, protractor, dividers, papers, message pads and other articles required by officers. However, in Normandy officers quickly tended not to wear any equipment that singled them out for snipers.

From Army Training Memorandum No 40 of August 1941.
A guide to the kit required by an officer engaged on active and mobile operations. Items of dress on the person are not included.

1 Items carried on the person

- ☐ AB153
- ☐ Binoculars
- ☐ Box of matches
- ☐ Cardigan (in haversack if not worn)
- ☐ Compass
- ☐ Emergency rations (as issued)
- ☐ *Field Service Pocket Book*
- ☐ Field dressing
- ☐ Gloves
- ☐ Identity discs
- ☐ Knife, fork and spoon
- ☐ Map case
- ☐ Mess tin and cover
- ☐ Technical books or instruments to arm of service
- ☐ Pay advance book (AFW 3241)
- ☐ Pistol and ammunition
- ☐ Pocket knife
- ☐ Protractor
- ☐ Ration bag
- ☐ Steel helmet
- ☐ Set of web equipment
- ☐ Torch
- ☐ Wristwatch
- ☐ Whistle and lanyard
- ☐ Waterbottle

- ☐ Anti-gas equipment
- ☐ Cape
- ☐ Cotton waste
- ☐ Individual detectors
- ☐ Eyeshields
- ☐ Ointment
- ☐ Respirator

2 Carried in pack or haversack

- ☐ Cap comforter
- ☐ FS cap
- ☐ Greatcoat
- ☐ Housewife
- ☐ Mug
- ☐ Spare socks, etc
- ☐ Scarf
- ☐ Spare laces and buttons
- ☐ Washing and shaving kit (incl. soap in tin box)

3 Baggage

- ☐ Bedding (sleeping bag recommended)
- ☐ Towels, 2
- ☐ Battledress
- ☐ Shirt
- ☐ Vest
- ☐ Drawers
- ☐ Boots
- ☐ Shoes or slippers
- ☐ Canvas bucket
- ☐ Small mirror (may be in pack)
- ☐ Writing materials
- ☐ Sundries

for WOs, NCOs and ORs were produced in *Regulations for the Clothing of the Army* (Clothing Regulations) produced in May 1936. Clothing Regulations were amended seven times between January 1937 and October 1939. They were republished in 1941 and 1943 as *War Clothing Regulations*.

Temperate climate uniforms
Battledress

When war was declared in 1939 the introduction of a new (1937) 'battledress' (BD) made from a hard-wearing wool worsted serge and a new range of webbing equipment (made from cotton that was waterproofed and dyed before being woven) which was smaller but less bulky than that worn in the First World War was still in progress. The mixed green and brown fibres of the serge matched the colours of the UK's vegetation and blended in better than a monochrome fabric. Issues of the new khaki BD were not completed until the end of 1940, although most of the BEF that was sent to France was so equipped. It consisted of a short-waisted blouse which was worn fastened up to the neck with a series of buttons and two concealed hooks and eyes at the collar, except for officers, who wore it open at the neck with a matching khaki collar and tie. The jacket had buttoned shoulder epaulettes and fastened down the front with five buttons, normally hidden by a fly front (although on later 'economy' versions the buttons were made from plastic or vegetable nut and uncovered), while the two breast patch pockets usually had box pleats and concealed buttons. The integral half-belt did up from left to right and fastened on the right hip with a built-in buckle of dull metal. The straight trousers had a capacious map pocket on the front of the left thigh, conventional slashed side pockets, a single right hip pocket with a pointed flap and a concealed button, and four spaced belt loops for use with the web belt when in shirt-sleeve order. The trousers were normally worn with boots and webbing gaiters, rather than puttees. The OR shirt was collarless. Some officers had their battledress tailored, so that the folded-back portions of the collar, which normally showed the sandy-coloured lining, were covered with pieces of khaki serge.

ABOVE These two Canadian soldiers show off their BD and a Nazi flag they captured in Mesnil. Taken in the sunshine on 10 August 1944, the men are from the Queen's Own Cameron Highlanders of Canada, 6th Infantry Brigade, 2nd Canadian Infantry Division.

LEFT Our reenactor corporal wears BD, full 1937 webbing with gas mask slung and a sizeable GS shovel. Note the toggle rope – more usually associated with commandos and paras. The long debates and experimentation with uniforms during the 1930s led to the adoption of the new BD, which had not completely been introduced by the time the BEF went to France. The BD went through some wartime changes (most notably to the collar which proved rough and uncomfortable). Liners were allowed from 3 April 1940.

With minor variations this remained the British Army's regular combat uniform until the 1960s.

Service Dress

The British Army's service dress (SD) was originally the combat uniform worn in the First World War that was replaced by the new BD. It was then retained for use outside combat or full ceremony. While all peacetime dress or parade uniforms, blue patrols (undress uniforms for use in barracks and off-duty wear for out of camp) etc, had generally been put away during the wartime years, officers were still permitted to wear SD for office duty or 'walking out'. This uniform resembled the officers' uniform of the First World War and was made of good-quality barathea (a fine woollen cloth, sometimes mixed with silk or cotton), the tunic being single-breasted, with shoulder straps, patched pockets, open (tailored) at the neck to show the matching shirt, collar and tie. Trousers were made from the same material, although some officers were entitled to wear riding breeches of cavalry twill, kilts or trews (Scottish regiments only). Normal headgear was the khaki SD cap, although some regiments would wear their own particular form of headdress such as the RTR's black beret. Service dress has continued in use to this day as an alternative between the combat uniform and full dress.

Headgear

Initially, the OR wore a sidecap of khaki serge, also known as a forage cap or a 'for and aft' for obvious reasons. It had been designed so that in cold weather it could be undone to protect the ears and part of the face, buttoning over the chin, but this was only partly successful and most soldiers did not like wearing it in this way, preferring to wear the stocking-type 'balaclava' for winter wear instead. The stiff OR SD-type cap was also seldom worn, except by the Corps of Military Police (CMP), whose caps had red tops, and some drill instructors in training establishments, who sometimes 'broke' the peak so that it was closer to and shadowed the eyes. By far the greatest headwear revolution came when the RTR-type beret was adopted by all regiments, although only the RAC wore

ABOVE AND BELOW Designed and patented by John Brodie in 1915, the helmets worn by most soldiers at the start of the war were of similar design and designated Helmet, Steel, Mark I* (with new chinstrap and liner) or Mk II (the latter with non-magnetic rim and later redesigned No 1 Mk I). The 3in mortar crew in the desert are wearing Mk IIs, whereas the Canadian corporal guarding German prisoners near Bernières-sur-Mer is wearing a Mk III (or turtle) helmet.

black berets. Paratroops wore red berets and most of the infantry pale khaki berets (in most units by 1943), Scottish regiments still retained Balmoral tam o'shanters or Glengarry bonnets, even in action. The most universal headgear worn in combat was of course the steel helmet, whose bowl-shaped appearance dated back to the Brodie helmet of the First World War. The 1938 Mk I and Mk II were the two most used in the Second World War, the differences between the two being the new anti-magnetic shell of the Mk II, with both sharing the new liner and chinstrap introduced in the updated Mk I. Helmets could be worn uncovered, with a string net in which to put natural or artificial camouflage, or with a full hessian cover. New M1944 Mk III helmets, shaped more like a tortoise shell and providing better lower head protection, were issued in time for D-Day and widely used thereafter. Only the RAS and the airborne forces wore other types of steel helmet, which were closer fitting. Other Commonwealth nations bought the British helmets and produced their own versions when supply problems curtailed availability and the US also at first copied the Mk I Brodie until the issue of their own M1 combat helmet in 1941.

Protective clothing

A new heavy woollen khaki greatcoat had been issued in 1939 to replace the previous 1909 single-breasted pattern that had been standard issue. It was mid-calf length and double-breasted with four pairs of brass buttons at the front and a two-buttoned vent at the rear. A belt secured with three smaller brass buttons allowed the volume of the coat to be adjusted by being pulled back inside via two reinforced slots. It also had button-fastened epaulettes, peaked lapels, plain cuffs and two hand warmer pockets with flaps. Problems with the new greatcoat fitting over other equipment and hanging evenly at the front necessitated an updated 1941 Pattern that was 2in shorter than that of 1939, with a long inverted vertical pleat down the back to increase expansion, a thicker lining on the shoulders and a slightly narrower and now button-fastened collar. The other major change was to be the addition of a 'jigger' button inside the coat to help support the weight of the material and keep the two front parts hanging evenly together. The buttons were also changed from brass to a green plastic or vegetable ivory (made from the tagua nut palm). The 1939 Pattern was never withdrawn

FAR LEFT AND LEFT
The 1939 greatcoat was double-breasted with a vent at the back (as seen far left). In 1941 the greatcoat was modified, shortened by 2in, given a pleat at the back and warmer lining. The weight of an infantryman's clothing and equipment is always a serious consideration: too much and items will be discarded (the Americans were notorious for this) or soldiers will be incapacitated; too little and they will run out of necessities too quickly. The 1937 pattern web equipment pamphlet gives the following weights for the infantryman's basic load:

(a) Articles of equipment 4lb 7.25oz (2kg);

(b) Articles carried in equipment 21lb 3.25oz (9.6kg);

(c) Clothing 11lb 11oz (5.3kg) - add 2lb 3.75oz (1kg) for large men, 2lb 3oz (just under 1kg) if steel helmet is worn and 2lb 7oz (1.1kg) if anti-gas cape is carried;

(d) Arms 9lb (4kg, rifle) or 13lb (5.9kg, Bren gun);

(e) Pack and contents 9lb 12oz (4.4kg). Total (battle order without pack) 46lb 5.5oz (21kg).

ABOVE **Well-armed infantrymen of the Lincoln and Welland Regiment, wearing snow camouflage clothing and life preservers, photographed the day after the fighting on the island of Kapelsche Veer in the Maas – Operation Elephant, 1 February 1945.** *(Lt H. Gordon Aikman/ Library and Archives Canada PA-144706)*

RIGHT **Rear view of the snow suit.**

FAR RIGHT **1930s experiments with uniform also led to the adoption of 1939 universal pattern denims which could be worn over BD. As illustrated here, they were slightly modified in 1940 with an improved blouse belt to stop slipping.**

and both versions continued to be used concurrently throughout the war.

Officers also wore the greatcoat, a trench coat (a shorter, more rainproof commercial coat for officers originating in the First World War) or else the beige 'British Warm', the latter being fundamentally similar to the issued greatcoat but privately manufactured from a higher-quality, heavy taupe Melton woollen fabric with a brown silk satin lining. Other favourites for cold weather wear were the old First World War collarless and sleeveless leather trench waistcoat. The normal rainwear was the rubberised waterproof

Mk VII Brown Cape. With 18 holes punched around its circumference, it could be used as a groundsheet or rain shelter. It was grouped at one corner with four extra buttons and a collar with a wrap-over flap so it could also be used as a rudimentary rain cape, with the centre of the back slightly hollowed to allow for a small pack to be worn. It must be said that it was not particularly effective in any of its assigned roles, and dispatch riders and the like had fuller and sturdier protective clothing. Finally, for armoured soldiers a tank oversuit (usually called a tank suit) was introduced from the summer of 1943 – this was warm, waterproof and comfortable, although the rain always collected in the crotch when in the sitting position like driving! Along with such cold weather clothing, warm woollen khaki pullovers, scarves and gloves or mittens were all worn.

Denims were considered as protective clothing, to be worn primarily by those doing dirty jobs, although in summer, two-piece and one-piece denims were often worn in combat, especially by tank and AFV crews. Denims had eight external pockets – two large breast pockets, two side pockets, two knee pockets, a hip pocket and a first field dressing pocket. They fastened with a concealed button front, a cloth belt and cloth straps at the end of the

ABOVE AND ABOVE RIGHT Sturdy, with four buttons and a blanket lining, the leather jerkin was warm in winter and very hard-wearing. Note the Fifth (US) Army insignia and the point-up chevron on the lower left arm of the reenactor. These good conduct stripes (granted after 2/6/12/18 years' service without formal discipline) also came with better pay. The maximum number was set at five.

BELOW Capt Vere-Hodge's Forward Observation Bombardment team, June 1944. Left to right: Telegraphists W. Fortune and A.J. Boomer, RN, DSM (note his Royal Navy shoulder insignia), Capt Francis Vere-Hodge, MC and Telegraphist K.F. Moles. Both Boomer and Vere-Hodge won medals for their work during the invasion of Sicily as part of a new formation, No 1 Combined Operations Bombardment Unit (COBU), formed to provide forward observation parties to direct naval gunfire on to shore targets. The COBUs mixed RA captains with RN signallers experienced in high-speed Morse communication, some delivered by air and others by sea. His party – one of 42 COBU teams allocated to the assault units in Operation Neptune, six of which were allocated to 6th Airborne – left from Fairford and landed at Ranville. Hodge used the lighthouse at Ouistreham as an OP, at first designated to link with the cruiser HMS *Mauritius*. Naval gunfire played an important role in Normandy and one of Vere-Hodge's final shoots was with the battleship *Ramillies*, which engaged targets only 200yd from Allied troops. All (other than Boomer) are wearing Denison smocks, modified Airborne BD trousers with expanded map pockets on the left leg and Parachute Regiment berets.

legs, plus internal braces and shoulder straps for rank badges.

Specialist clothing

The airborne forces in particular needed specialist clothing, such as jump jackets and Denison smocks, which were made of extra-strong, camouflaged material and incorporated zips or heavy duty snap-fasteners. Both were windproof and showerproof, but the latter became waterlogged in heavy rain. Nevertheless they were highly prized. A third garment – the airborne forces (sleeveless) oversmock – was issued later in the war but was not in general service until just before D-Day.

Hospital clothing

'Hospital Blues' were issued to in-patients at military hospitals and comprised a royal blue serge jacket and matching trousers, plus a white shirt and red tie. All were made of inferior material and badly tailored, to the chagrin of their now twice-wounded wearers. Some similar-coloured tropical hospital clothing was also issued for use in hotter climates.

ABOVE General Auchinleck, Commander-in-Chief of the Middle East Forces, inspecting men of the 2nd New Zealand Expeditionary Force at Baggush near Mersa Matruh on 4 November 1941 – the eve of the Libyan campaign. To the left, Brig Lindsay Merritt Inglis and Gen Bernard Freyberg. The troops are wearing khaki drill uniforms with hose tops and short puttees, FS caps and 37 Pattern webbing.

RIGHT This soldier takes a moment to read a locally produced forces newspaper (the *Tripoli Times*, first issue dated 23 January 1943) and have a mug of tea from the NAAFI. He wears typical uniform for those in North Africa consisting of khaki drill cotton shorts, made in the UK, and an Indian-produced Aertex shirt. He wears the same field service cap as men back in Britain, despite it offering little protection from the sun. Like his shirt, his 37 Pattern webbing was made in India and shipped to North Africa – the shorter supply lines and not having to pass through the Mediterranean made this a sensible route. He has slung his SMLE over his shoulder and an enamelled mug hangs from his small pack. *(Ed Hallett)*

Khaki Drill and Jungle Green

BD was clearly too hot for normal daywear in the Middle East and Far East, but desert nights were often bitterly cold once the sun had set, as were numerous mountainous areas of Tunisia. Thus, BD was worn on occasions and greatcoats, sheepskin coats and the like were widely used. Instead suitable 'Khaki Drill' and 'Jungle Green' uniforms were worn. Khaki Drill (KD) uniforms were evolved by the British Army in India, using lighter cloths and Indian cottons to make tunics, shirts, long trousers and shorts, to be worn with boots or shoes. In the 1930s KD also incorporated British Aertex in its bush shirts and jackets and by 1939 British troops wore pale tan KD shorts or trousers with long-sleeved Aertex shirts and jackets with pleated chest pockets and scalloped flaps, lower bellows pockets which were also flapped, rank epaulettes, long sleeves with a buttoning cuff and a matching waist belt and brass buckle. One of the most unpopular of the tropical items were the KD shorts with extra deep turn-ups, worn either buttoned up or let down to be bound round the ankles with special threaded white tapes, thus eliminating the need to wear KD trousers. They were a disaster when issued early on in North Africa and did not last long, being known as 'Bombay Bloomers'. By and large KD kit worked fine in the desert and later in the Mediterranean theatre's summer, but in the damp jungles of the Far East they required a redesign more than just being dyed 'Jungle Green' (JG). After much research the 1943 JG BD was

LEFT British, West African and Gurkha troops wait to board a DC-3 to move to Broadway during the Wingate–Cochran Expedition. This second operation saw gliders used to deliver the Chindits behind enemy lines from where they disrupted the Japanese offensive. While the usefulness of the Chindits has been questioned, the Japanese thought them significant. The men are wearing Indian-made JG BD. The anklets look like they are of Indian origin and have leather straps and reinforcing to help them stand up to jungle conditions a little longer. They all have wool-felt slouch hats. Note the man with a rifle grenade launcher attached to his rifle in the centre of the shot.

ABOVE This Royal Engineer lieutenant is taking a breather with a cup of hot sweet 'char'. Most of his uniform and equipment is Indian-made by this point, including the JG BD, JG webbing, mess tin and water bottle, his anklets and even his mug. His jungle hat and machete are British-made, as is his newly issued Lee-Enfield No 5 'jungle carbine'.
(Ed Hallett)

ABOVE A jungle patrol on 6 November 1944. Covered by a Bren gun – just visible in front of the man with the SMLE – a patrol advances into the banana trees led by a soldier with a Thompson SMG. They are wearing JG BD with 37 Pattern webbing, possibly Indian in origin. They wear Mk II steel helmets and the man on the right has added a compass pouch to his standard rifleman's webbing.

BELOW What a member of 2/EYorks might have carried on D-Day. In his right hand he holds the inflatable life preserver. This had to be worn with care as it could easily pitch the wearer over into a position from which he would find it hard to right himself. He has a gas mask on his chest, a turtle Mk III helmet, SMLE and bandoleer. He also wears a battle jerkin. Designed by Colonel E.R. Rivers-Macpherson, RAOC, Chief Ordnance Officer, Aldershot, it sought to replace the 1937 webbing that Rivers-Macpherson thought clumsy and restricted movement. Made from waterproof canvas in three sizes (L/M/S) and in four colours (tan, white, brown and green for desert, snow, spring/summer European and Pacific uses, respectively) it had multiple pockets – the two at the front to carry Bren magazines – side bomb pockets, sleeve for the machete, No 4 bayonet and entrenching tool helve, lower pouch with entrenching tool head. The various fastenings are primarily by toggle and the jerkin was designed to be easier to carry in combat. The main criticism of the battle jerkin was that it led to overheating in action.

produced, consisting of an Aertex blouse and hard-wearing drill trousers, but the blouse was soon dismissed by the troops as being too light, uncomfortable and impractical, with a tendency to ride up even more readily than the original wool BD blouse. Where possible it was replaced by a longer, four-pocket JG Aertex bush shirt, or the more comfortable and popular two-pocket Indian wool (flannel) shirt. Headgear such as slouch hats were issued for jungle wear, but in the Middle East most soldiers wore their normal regimental hats, berets, or in action, steel helmets. Other necessary clothing items such as long stockings, hose tops, thin vests and pants etc, were issued to all ranks as necessary.

Peculiar dress items

In the desert many officers wore hard-wearing corduroy trousers, desert boots (suede with crepe rubber soles – universally known as 'Brothel Creepers'), coloured silk scarves and so on. This continued in some formations even when they had left North Africa (eg 7th Armd Div), although it must be said that this was

ABOVE Haversack contents: mess tins and 24-hour ration pack, shaving kit, Housewife, wool jumper, spare socks, cap comforter, white cotton towel.

(Ed Hallett)

always a prerogative enjoyed by officers and the occasional warrant officer, not the average OR. Monty was always an individual dresser – photos of him in Normandy show him wearing corduroy trousers, a sheepskin flying jacket and an RTR beret.

Personal equipment

Each man was issued with two packs, termed Large and Small, both being simple webbing bags with flap tops fastened by two narrow webbing straps and buckles – a haversack and pack. The haversack was worn on the back and would normally contain a few personal belongings, a water bottle, mess tins, emergency rations, cigarettes and chocolate, a knife, fork and spoon set, a cardigan, water-sterilising outfit, a balaclava and, last of all, a waterproof sheet or anti-gas cape under the main flap to help keep out the rain.

BELOW Shaving kit: mirror and case, shaving gear, soap dish, toothbrush, button slide.

The pack would usually be carried on the platoon truck and would contain an extra pair of socks and laces, one cap comforter, one soft cap, one roll-up holdall containing shaving and other personal equipment, a bar of soap, one towel, one 'Housewife' (as the name implies this was a small sewing/darning kit carried by all soldiers so that they could repair minor tears, sew on buttons, darn holes in socks, etc) and the soldier's greatcoat when not in use. Each man would also carry 50 rounds of ammunition for his weapon and perhaps a few grenades in his webbing pouches. The 1937 Pattern webbing had been developed from the 1908 Pattern but was far lighter and had been designed to suit all arms – not just the infantry. It was made from pre-shrunk cotton webbing that had been waterproofed and dyed before being woven and its fittings were made of stamped brass. However, it was still designed to accept blanco and its brass fittings allowed to dull when in action, but were polished for parades. Apart from the bayonet, no articles were suspended below the wearer's waistline so as not to impede movement.

Deficiencies were identified with 1937 Pattern webbing, particularly in the Far East, and in 1943 the Lethbridge Mission was sent there to identify where improvements could be made. This led to the 1944 Pattern Web Equipment. It was lightweight webbing, using alloy metal and incorporating such items as the excellent US-type water bottle and cup. The new webbing was dyed Jungle Green with dulled metal fittings. However, this webbing didn't reach the field before the war's end.

The basic harness was as follows: a belt (approximately 2.5in wide) joined by a patent buckle; two web pouches 'universal', to be fixed on the front of the belt, each of which could accommodate Bren magazines, rifle ammunition clips, or No 36 grenades; two braces that went up under the BD shoulder straps to cross at the back and be attached to buckles at the rear of the belt. A bayonet frog, an entrenching tool (from 1942) that had a head and separate handle, both conveyed in a carrier, and a water-bottle/canteen were other items carried.

Anti-gas equipment

The General Service Respirator (GSR) Mk IV came in three sizes (small, normal and large) and was designed to allow the wearer to withstand heavy concentrations of gas for long periods, while allowing the greatest possible freedom of movement and comfort. Consisting of a mask with a hose connected to the filter, it rode in a waterproof canvas haversack that stored the whole device when not in use. The Mk IV was made out of high-quality rubber sometimes coated with a canvas stockinette and had two large glass triple-layered eye pieces held in place with metal rings. The valves and the speech diaphragm (to enable the wearer to speak) were placed in a cast-aluminium housing, to which the fixed hose also connected and the mask fastened using a basic six-point harness system with a small rubber patch in the centre. The filters themselves were made up predominantly of oxidised charcoal, but also contained crocidolite (blue asbestos) filtering pads, which at the time was not known to be carcinogenic. When in use, the haversack was worn at the front mounted on the chest. When carried stored, the respirator was returned to the haversack, the main part of which was divided into two – one part for the container, the other for the facepiece and anti-dimming outfit. These were supplied with the service respirator and fitted in a loop to the bottom of the haversack. It came with cloth one end and paste in the other, with the anti-dimming compound to be applied to the insides of the

ABOVE LEFT Compare this reverse view with that of the D-Day battle jerkin on page 103. Here the soldier carries a pick and three mortar bombs.

ABOVE 1937 Pattern webbing manufactured in India for these troops of the Rajput Regiment. Two of the regiment's five battalions (the 3rd and 4th) fought in the Middle East, the latter returning to fight at Kohima after El Alamein. The 5th was captured when Hong Kong fell, and the other two battalions fought on the Arakan front.

BELOW This back view of a Canadian corporal in Normandy shows typical webbing layout with shovel inserted at right angles to its normal vertical position – many soldiers found the upright stowage interfered with their helmets. *(Library and Archives Canada)*

RIGHT In spite of the fact that it wasn't used by Germany or the Allies in the Second World War, gas was always a threat – and one that many remembered from the First World War. The gas cape was the first line of defence. It was designed to be able to fit over the webbing and pack. It was often used as a raincoat.

eyepieces. This made moisture form – not a mist but a clear film which did not interfere with vision. The correct application of anti-dimming compound was an important part of the respirator drill, and careful attention was paid to it. The haversack had a canvas carrying sling and a length of stout cord attached, which was used when the respirator was being worn in the alert position on the chest, being tied around the upper part of the waist. In 1943 a new respirator was issued, known as 'Respirator, Anti-Gas, Light' as it was about half the weight and bulk of the earlier model and was held in a much smaller carrier.

Other items of general issue anti-gas equipment included anti-gas capes, carried attached to the haversack or worn across the shoulders for quick access. The capes originally came in tan, then olive brown, chocolate and finally camouflage versions. Soldiers soon found that these made excellent raincoats – much better than the issued rainwear. There were also more specialised items including hoods, overboots and gloves, to prevent gas contact with skin and possible severe burns, but these were issued separately as extras. In the event gas was not an issue for the troops, who began to dispose of the masks and use the haversack for carrying other things. Field dressings and additional medical kit such as elastoplast bound around a pencil, lint and scissors were also often carried in the gas mask case.

Miscellaneous items
Identity discs
All serving soldiers were issued with a set of fibre identity discs – a green disc (No 1) and a red disc (No 2) – and a 3ft length of thin cord. Both were worn around the neck under the shirt, with the red disc on a separate extension piece of the cord so that it could be removed. There was a second red disc issued separately that was attached to the soldier's service respirator. The discs worn by the soldier showed his army number, initials, surname in full and his religious denomination (CE = Church of England, RC = Roman Catholic, etc). The red disc was removed before burial to assist in identification, but the green disc was never to be removed. Unfortunately, it was found that the fibre discs lost their markings, especially in the intense heat of an AFV 'brew up', while the cord burnt away. Therefore the use of jungle issue stainless steel ID discs and nylon cord were issued, but were still not as good as their US Army equivalents.

First field dressings
Carried in battle by every soldier, first field dressings were the first line of treatment for the freshly wounded intended for use by the wounded man himself or his comrades and were carried in an internal pocket of the service dress jacket or in a special pocket in the BD/KD shorts or trousers. They consisted of a small khaki or brown fabric bag containing two dressings of waterproof gauze and cotton wool bandage and two safety pins. In the UK the issue was restricted (for example, to NCOs, MT drivers, those attending battle schools or major exercise) and held in bulk in company/battalion stores, to be issued as and when ordered.

Eating utensils, etc
In addition to a water bottle, each man was issued with a pair of rectangular mess tins with folding carrying handles, one slightly smaller than the other so that they could be stowed together (prewar ones were made of aluminium alloy, wartime manufacture was in tinplate). A highly modified version was manufactured in Australia based on the UK Pattern 37 design. It had approximately the same width and length,

This top-break double-action revolver was the official service pistol for the British military in the Second World War. It could fire single shots or was capable of rapid fire by trigger action. Used primarily by officers, during the later stages of the war they were targeted by snipers because of the pistol, so badges of rank were covered or removed and the pistol was replaced by a rifle. Accuracy was its main problem – hitting a target was down to luck rather than judgement, particularly at distance.

Webley Mk IV Revolver

Calibre: .38in (9.65mm)
In service: From 1942
Variants: Various, Mk VI (calibre .455in) also used in the Second World War
Designed: Webley & Scott Ltd, Birmingham
Manufacturers: Webley & Scott Ltd, Birmingham
Number produced: c126,000
Weight: 2lb 6.5oz (1.1kg)
Overall length: 10.25in (26cm)
Barrel length: 5in (12.75cm), seven grooves right-hand twist
Ammunition: 200 grain
Rate of fire: 20–30pm but with the same problem as the Enfield No 2 Mk I Revolver
Muzzle velocity: 620ft/sec (190m/sec)
Sights: Notch rear sight and blade/post front
Range: 150ft (45.72m).

BELOW **The Webley Mk IV .38/200 Service Revolver was another top-break weapon and, following the inability of RSAF Enfield to produce sufficient quantities of the Enfield No 2, it was adopted in 1942.** *(Simon Clay/Greene Media)*

Classic revolver shape: large frame, Bakelite grips with Webley logo but with a unique barrel design adopted by Enfield. Made in quantity by Webley & Scott because they were in short supply and to take pressure off RSAF, Enfield. Often used by tank and armoured crews and units more likely to be involved with close-quarter fighting, such as commandos, paratroops and special forces. This top-break double-action revolver was easy to load: thumb the latch and press, thus opening the revolver, and then drop in six rounds and close. The cases were self-extracting when the pistol was broken (opened). As with the Enfield, accuracy was a problem.

Colt M1911A1 Automatic Pistol

Calibre: .45in (11.4mm)
In service: 1911–80s
Variants: The A1 was an M1911 produced from 1924 after a number of modifications
Designed: Original design by John Browning in 1908, with Colt's design accepted by the US Army in 1911
Manufacturers: Colt Patent Firearms, Remington Arms, Springfield Armory and others
Number produced: 2.7 million (of which 1.9 million in the United States)
Weight: 2lb 7oz (1.22kg) loaded
Overall length: 8.5in (21.6cm)
Barrel length: 5in (12.7cm), six grooves left-hand twist
Ammunition: 230 grain
Rate of fire: Rapid when needed but with loss of accuracy
Muzzle velocity: 830ft/sec (253m/sec)
Sights: Blade front and V rear
Range: 150ft (45.72m) effective.

The most powerful pistol in service, this American classic was a man-stopper with the size and weight of the round doing the damage – but accuracy was only possible if it was fired at close range. A single-action, semi-automatic, short recoil-operated, magazine-fed pistol, its magazine was a seven-round box inserted into the pistol grip. A catch on the left-hand side of the grip released the magazine. To eject a round still in the chamber, pull back the breech slide. All branches of the Allies' military forces used it, including British airborne, commandos and special forces.

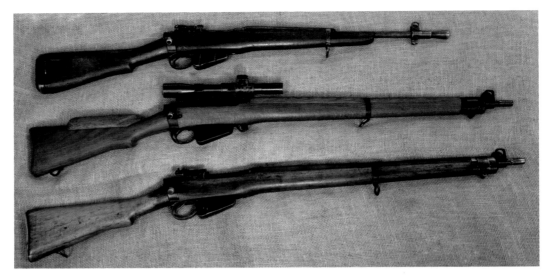

Rifles

Short Magazine Lee-Enfield Rifle

Calibre: .303in (modified in the 1970s to take the NATO 7.62mm round)

In service: With many variations, from 1895 as the Model Lee-Enfield (MLE) and then as the better-known SMLE from 1904 to today, especially in the Indian subcontinent. It was retained by the British until the mid-1960s as the L42A1 7.62mm Sniper variant

Variants: Mks I, II, III, III*; Mk V trial only; No 4

Mk I from 1941, Mk I* from 1942; No 5 Mk I Jungle Carbine with a shorter barrel

Designed: James P. Lee (magazine and bolt system) and the RSAF Enfield

Manufacturers: RSAF Enfield, BSA-Shirley, ROF Fazakerley, LSAC Ltd and the USA, Canada and other Commonwealth nations

Number produced: In excess of 1.7 million of all variants

Weight: SMLE – 8.73lb (3.96kg); No 4 – 9.06lb (4.11kg); No 5 – 7lb 1oz (3.20kg)

Overall length: SMLE – 44.5in (1.132m); No 4 – 44.45in (1.129m); No 5 – 39.5in (1.003m)

Barrel length: SMLE – 25.2in (640mm); No 4 – 25.2in (640mm); No 5 – 18.8in (480mm)

Ammunition: .303in rimmed ball, tracer, AP and incendiary (developed in the First World War by the Brock family, still producing fireworks today). These rounds were colour-coded: ball, purple; tracer, red; AP, green; incendiary, blue

Feed: Lee bolt-action feed from a ten-round column-fed box magazine charged by five-round stripper clips. These were pushed into the magazine via an open bolt. The removable magazine could be preloaded but this was rarely done as it was too time consuming. (Little changes in the army – when the SA80 replaced the SLR, poor design meant that the SA80 magazine could drop off: a very serious offence in Northern Ireland. Richard Charlton-Taylor reports having used paracord to ensure his mag stayed attached to his SA80!)

Rate of fire: 20–30 aimed shots per minute was expected from regular infantry. The

BELOW Enschede, Netherlands, 3 April 1945 – a Canadian soldier keeps a careful eye on surrendering Germans. He's togged up for the cold with woollen gloves and a well-worn windproof smock, has a 'pigsticker' bayonet on his Lee-Enfield No 4 and a knife in his gaiter. *(Nationaalarchief.nl)*

legendary 'mad minute', however, was more myth than reality, although in 1914 38 rounds hit a 12-in target at 300yd

Muzzle velocity: 2,441ft/sec (744m/sec) subject to type of round

Sights: Protected blade foresight. The rear sights were initially a sliding ramp, then a fixed and adjustable aperture sights on later versions.

Range: 300yd battle sights; 2,000yd max effective.

The rear-locking fast-action rifle bolt cocked on closing. Rapid fire allowed the Lee bolt system to be palm-cocked and loaded while keeping line of sight and finger pressure on the trigger. The personal weapon of the British or Commonwealth rifleman from 1904, it is still used today. Robust and reliable, it was soldier-proof and without weaknesses. It had a range of accessories and attachments:

- Cleaning kit with brass oil container in butt slot and pull-through with gauze in web pouch
- Canvas sling and muzzle cover
- Bayonet: SMLE – 1907 12-in blade; No 4 Mk I and onwards assorted spike bayonets and some bladed
- HT – heavy barrel telescopic sight developed by the Australians and selected No 4 rifles with adjustable cheekpiece and mounts for a No 32 3.5× telescopic sight. Each scope and mount was matched to a specific rifle. NB: sniper rifles are not interchangeable between snipers.

ABOVE The Lee-Enfield No 4 Mk I(T) was the sniper's version and these four men from the Queen's Own Cameron Highlanders of Canada had been putting their telescopic sights to good use. The wartime caption identifies the men as having killed 101 of the enemy through sniping operations since D-Day. This photograph was taken at Camp de Brasschaat, Belgium, 9 October 1944. *(Lt Ken Bell/Library and Archives Canada PA-138416)*

SMGs

Sten Submachine Gun

Calibre: 9mm

In service: 1941 until replaced in the British Army by the Sterling in the late 1950s and 1960s; still in service with many armies worldwide

Variants: Mk I (original version had wooden foregrip and conical flash hider), Mk I*, Mk II (most produced version; a slightly longer Mk II was produced in Canada), Mk III, Mk V (the Mk IV wasn't put into production). There

BELOW Sten Mk III with rod stock and sling. Designed to be cheap to mass-produce, the Sten may not have been the most accurate infantry weapon of the Second World War, and was prone to jam, but it provided more firepower than a rifle and was used extensively by airborne forces and SOE as well as being issued to almost everyone who didn't carry a rifle or a Bren gun. *(Simon Clay/ Greene Media)*

were a number of suppressed versions (Mk IIS and Mk VI) and many minor variations/modifications

Designed: Maj R.V. Shepherd, Harold Turpin and Enfield. Thus the acronym S T EN

Manufacturers: RSAF Enfield, ROF Fazakerley, BSA, Lines Bros (makers of Triang toys – the Mk III). Also made in Canada at Long Branch Arsenal, Ontario

Number produced: In excess of 4.5 million of all types

Weight: 6lb 8oz to 8lb (2.95–3.62kg)

Overall length: Mk II – 30in (76.2cm); others subject to type of stock

Barrel length: 7.7in (19.68cm)

Ammunition: 9mm round-nose pistol, based on the German Parabellum Luger round of 1902. ('*Si vis pacem, para bellum*' translates from the Latin as 'if you want/seek peace prepare for war'.) Some 110 million rounds ordered from the USA to allow British manufacturers to tool up for production

Feed: Double column to single feed, detachable 32-round box magazine, but usually only 30 rounds inserted to ease pressure on the spring

Rate of fire: Cyclic 500–550 rounds/min

Muzzle velocity: 1,425ft/sec (434m/sec), subject to mark and variations. The suppressed (silenced) variant fired at 1,000ft/sec (305m/sec)

Sights: Fixed post front and fixed aperture 'peep' sights at rear

Range: 150ft (45.7m) effective; 600ft (183m) max.

First used in any numbers by Canadian forces at Dieppe in 1942, the air-cooled Sten was used as a personal weapon in place of the harder-to-get Thompson. Cheap and easy to mass-produce for as little as £3–4 in the early 1940s, the Sten was a remarkable weapon for its time – desperate measures for desperate times. It could fire as a single shot or automatic, its blowback operating from an open bolt. It required no lubricant for its working parts. It was good for resistance groups – particularly with so much German 9mm ammunition readily available – and even the Germans copied it. It is still produced today. Accessories included a cleaning kit, a canvas cover for suppressed marks, a magazine-filling device and a sling and others subject to mark. There were various attachments: assorted stocks, foregrips and trigger guards made of wood or pressed steel of various types, and a bayonet could be attached. Its main weakness was that it was prone to magazine jams; indeed, shoddy working parts were easily jammed by conditions and location. It could be lethal if dropped – it can be cocked by dropping the stock end on to a mattress (from experience!).

Thompson Submachine Gun

Calibre: .45in (11.43mm)

In service: It was used by British and Commonwealth armies throughout the Second World War and beyond

Variants: M1919 – used by the New York Police Department. Not issued to the military; M1921 – first issue to the US military.

LEFT Another classic design, the Thompson SMG was built in huge numbers and used by most of the combatants during the Second World War, most of them taking the cheaper wartime models M1 and M1A1. Until replaced by the Sten, the Tommy gun equipped section leaders in the British Army, supplying good offensive fire. The photograph shows men of the New Zealand Corps who fought at Monte Cassino: when the New Zealand Division withdrew it had suffered 343 dead and over 600 wounded.

It was expensive and over-tooled, with a pistol grip and drum magazine; M1923 – not adopted by the military; M1921 AC – introduced in 1926, it incorporated the Cutts compensator (muzzle brake) as an option to counter recoil and muzzle rise when firing; M1928 – first major issue to US Army, Navy and Marine Corps, it had a slower cyclic rate of fire; M1928A1 – the pistol grip forend was replaced by a horizontal forend. It had a sling and options of 20-, 30- or 50-round drum magazine. It had cooling fins on the barrel, which were omitted on later marks to save money; M1A1 – further cost savings produced the M1A1, which became the standard SMG of the US military. It had a firing pin machined to the face of the bolt and a box magazine. Manufacturing costs were reduced from $210 in 1939 to $45 in 1944

Designed: Gen John T. Thompson, based on development of the limitations of the Blish principle, extreme friction metal on metal rather than the blowback or recoil-reloading system on many automatic weapons of the day

Manufacturers: Auto-Ordnance Company, Colt, Savage and BSA in the UK

Number produced: 1.75 million of all variants, the bulk built 1939–45

Weight: 10–10.8lb (4.5–4.9kg) unloaded

Overall length: 31.9–33.7in (81–86cm) with Cutts compensator

Barrel length: 10.52in (26.7cm) and 12in (30.5cm) with the Cutts

Ammunition: .45ACP (Automatic Colt Pistol). J.M. Browning designed this low-velocity round for the M1911 Colt

Feed: Originally drum magazines but these were prone to fouling, were too heavy and expensive to produce. The British military returned most of these in exchange for box magazines. The later marks had 20–30-round box magazines, which were easier to load and clear stoppages and one of the first to have a double-column double-feed magazine

Rate of fire: M1919 – 1,500 rounds/min, M1928 – 600–750 rounds/min. The heavier spring and actuator slowed the cyclic rate. M1A1 – 700–800 rounds/min

Muzzle velocity: 935ft/sec (285m/sec)

Sights: Blade front and the early model flip-up rear sight was replaced by a fixed L sight for later marks as well as triangular guard wings

Range: 480ft (149m) effective.

The Tommy gun was an individual weapon used by patrol leaders, NCOs, vehicle-mounted crew and fighting patrols, in close-quarter fighting and ambushes – in fact anyone who could get hold of one! It could be fired in semi- or fully automatic modes and operated by blowback, open bolt system held to the rear. Pressing the trigger and holding caused the bolt to chamber a round, fire it, eject the cartridge case and chamber another round until the trigger was released or the magazine empty. The cocking lever on early marks was on top of the receiver but on the M1A1 was on the side.

The weapon had a number of accessories: pistol foregrip, Cutts compensator, sling, drum or box magazines (the box magazine was easier to load) – a taped/welded double-magazine was developed for jungle warfare. Some marks had a removable buttstock.

This close-quarter weapon had a high rate of fire, was ideal for confined spaces and had good stopping power but its heavy, low-velocity round had poor penetration. It was an over-tooled weapon that was expensive to make, and was slow loading with a drum magazine.

ABOVE The Thompson was expensive to manufacture: the M1928A1 cost £50 to the Sten's £2.50. The Second World War production version, the M1A1 (of which over 1.5 million were built), was a simplified M1928A1 with a plain barrel, fixed butt and no compensator. It was heavy but did the job. (Simon Clay/Greene Media)

ABOVE New Britain, 4 April 1945. Pte Leon Ravet of Parramatta, New South Wales (left), and Pte Bernard Kentwell of Cronulla, New South Wales, on the alert while on patrol duty with their Owen machine carbines. Both men served with the 19th Bn, South Sydney Regiment, which was tasked with the defence of Darwin before moving to New Guinea and New Britain in 1941. Its magazine may look unwieldy but it was respected as being more reliable than the Sten or the Thompson and became known as the 'Digger's Darling'. It was designed by inventor Evelyn 'Evo' Owen in 1938 and was, as his hometown Wollongong, New South Wales proudly asserts, 'the only weapon entirely designed in Australia and was assembled right here in the Illawarra'. *(AWM)*

BELOW Lt Col Tucker, commanding officer of the 2/23 Infantry Battalion – one of the Australian units to have been besieged in Tobruk – testing a suppressed Austen in Borneo in September 1945. (Note also the suppressed Owen gun in the background.) *(AWM)*

Owen Machine Carbine

Calibre: 9mm Parabellum

In service: 1942 to early 1960s (ordnance officers weren't initially very positive and it needed radical redesign)

Variants: Mk 1 (1/42) – basic model with cooling fins on the barrel and a frame-type buttstock; Mk 1 (1/43) – no cooling fins and an all-wood butt; Mk 2 – change to butt and a bayonet, but only at prototype by end of the war; Mk 1 (1/44) – same as the Mk 1 (1/43) but with a bayonet

Designed: Lt Evelyn Owen had been working on a design during the 1930s which became more necessary when war broke out to meet the demand for an SMG which Britain could not supply

Manufacturers: Lysaght's Works, New South Wales. Lysaght's covered much of the production costs

Number produced: 45,000

Weight: 9.33lb (4.2kg) without magazine; 10.7lb (4.8kg) loaded

Overall length: 32in (81.3cm)

Barrel length: 9.8in (25cm), seven grooves right-hand twist

Ammunition: 9 × 19 Parabellum

Feed: Detachable vertical box magazine, gravity-fed, two-column type (when charging the magazine each round went slightly L or R). A post on the magazine ejected the cartridge case downwards

Rate of fire: 700 rounds/min

Muzzle velocity: 1,200ft/sec (366m/sec)

Sights: Peep rear sight and blade front

Range: 300ft (91.4m) effective; 660ft (200m) max.

The Owen gun was reliable and soldier proof. A more robust weapon than the Sten, it could withstand the harsh tropical conditions and was much liked – by US as well as Australian and New Zealand troops. Its drawbacks were that it was heavy, had a high rate of fire and a slow production time.

Austen Submachine Gun

Calibre: 9mm

In service: 1942–44

Variants: Mk I – based on the Mk II Sten and the German MP38; Mk II – with many

changes and modifications, although very few produced; suppressed version – for covert operations
Designed: By committee based on tried and tested systems
Manufacturers: Diecasters Ltd, Melbourne and W.J. Carmichael & Co., Melbourne
Number produced: 20,000
Weight: 8.8lb (3.98kg) unloaded
Length: 33.25in (84.45cm) stock open; 21.5in (55.2cm) stock folded
Barrel length: 7.75in (19.8cm)
Ammunition: 9 × 19 Parabellum
Feed: Side-loading 32-round Sten or Austen box magazine
Rate of fire: 500 rounds/min
Muzzle velocity: 1,200ft/sec (366m/sec)
Sights: Peep rear and triangle front
Range: 300ft (91.4m) effective; 660ft (200m) max.

The Australian Sten – used by the Australian and New Zealand armies – had a pistol-grip trigger and pistol-grip forend. The MP38 folding stock housed a screwdriver in one strut and a cleaning rod in the other. It had a blowback action and a side-mounted detachable box magazine. Unlike the Owen it could be mass-produced and was both well made and easy to handle. Its short bolt action made firing it more violent. Moving parts were sealed to prevent dirt entering the action. However, it was not popular as its exposed working parts were prone to fouling and the side-mounted magazine was a hindrance in the jungle. It was obsolete at the end of the war.

Machine guns

Bren Light Machine Gun
Calibre: .303in (7.7mm)
In service: 1938–80s. The Bren is still in use worldwide with variations in calibre, magazine and flash suppressor
Variants: Mk I (1937) – over-tooled with unnecessary attachments such as rear grip under the butt, dial rear sights and adjustable bipod; Mk II (1941) – simplified version of the Mk I. Basic woodwork and fewer milling operations; Mk III (1944) – shorter and lighter version for airborne and jungle warfare; Mk IV (1944) – Mk II converted to Mk III; L4 – various created postwar using the NATO 7.62 × 51 ammunition
Designed: Based on the Czech ZB vs.26 and modified as the ZGB 33 and then licensed for manufacture in the UK. Changes included a curved magazine for the rimmed .303in. Adopted by the British in 1935
Manufacturers: RSAF Enfield, John Inglis & Co. and Long Branch Canada, Lithgow in Australia and Ishapore in India
Number produced: Over 500,000 during wartime (split 55%/45% UK and Canada) – production still continues in India
Weight: Mk I/II – 22.82lb (10.35kg) without magazine; 25lb (11.25kg) with Mk III/IV – 19.15lb (8.68kg) without magazine; 21.6lb (9.75kg) with magazine
Overall length: 45in (115.6cm)

BELOW The main section weapon of the war for British and Commonwealth troops, the Bren was accurate, dependable and produced in large numbers, at one stage in 1940 exclusively at Enfield where a successful air raid could have caused big problems. *(Simon Clay/ Greene Media)*

ABOVE As the Germans built their section around the MG34 or MG42, so the British built theirs around the Bren. Its two-man team and a commander (usually a l/cpl) formed the gun group, while the whole section carried magazines for them and also were proficient in the gun's use.

BELOW The main element of the Bren No 2's kit was the spare barrel that had to be changed regularly when in constant use.

Barrel length: 25in (63.5cm)
Ammunition: Rimmed bottle neck – ball, tracer and incendiary
Feed: Detachable 30-round curved box magazine, though usually holding fewer to allow for grit and spring wear
Rate of fire: 450–500 rounds/min – single or automatic
Muzzle velocity: 2,440ft/sec (744m/sec)
Sights: Fixed forefront. Drum for Mk I/II, adjustable offset calibrated rear sight. Optical
Range: 1,500–1,800ft (457–548m) accurate; 3,000ft (914.5m) effective.

Named BREN from the initials of its two originating locations – BRno and ENfield – this was one of the best weapons of the war. It was gas-operated, venting down the barrel through a choice of four vents to push back a piston and breechblock. It could be one-man operated, although more usually with a crew of two: the No 1 was the gunner; the No 2 carried the spare barrel, tool kit and extra ammunition. He was responsible for loading and the important barrel-change that was essential if fire was sustained. Initial scale was one per rifle section but it was soon realised that this was insufficient and so all soldiers were trained in its operation. It was used in the direct- and indirect-fire role from hand, bipod or a tripod – there was an AA extendable tripod. Other than the tripod and bipod, there were many accessories including optics, cartridge case catchers and the loader's spare-barrel bag (which also contained a section's spares kit, including pull-through cord, oil bottles, cleaning brushes and tin with spares kit and gauges). There was also a sling that was used to support the weapon when advancing to contact or attacking.

Reliable and robust, air-cooled with easy barrel change, it had an adjustable gas regulator to increase pressure if the barrel was beginning to foul or if temperature was excessive. Extremely accurate, the use of a magazine prevented dirt from fouling the rounds as often happened with belt-fed machine guns – although this also meant its rate of fire was reduced as magazines had to be changed regularly. Spent cases ejected downward.

Anti-tank weapons

Boys Anti-tank Rifle

Calibre: .55in (13.99mm)

In service: 1937–43 with British and Commonwealth armies up until the end of the Desert War; Finland during the Winter War of 1939–40; also European and Far East Resistance groups

Variants: Mk I with a three-port circular muzzle brake and a T-shaped monopod; Mk II with a 'harmonica' squared muzzle brake and a bipod. There was an airborne version, calibre .30in (7.62mm), with no muzzle brake

Designed: Captain H.C. Boys at BSA and RSAF Enfield

Manufacturers: BSA and RSAF Enfield; John Inglis & Co., Canada

Number produced: About 114,000 by 1943 with nearly 50,000 exported

Weight: 36lb (16kg) without magazine; 38.5lb (17.50kg) with loaded magazine

Overall length: 62in (1.57m); 56in (1.42m) airborne version

Barrel length: 48in (91cm); 30in (76.2cm) airborne version

Ammunition: Kynoch Mk I rimless, which could penetrate armoured cars and halftracks; Mk II – a lighter APCR round with increased propellant based on the tungsten carbide-cored German version

Feed: 5-round top-feed detachable box magazine

Rate of fire: 10 rounds/min

Muzzle velocity: Mk I – 2,450ft/sec (747m/sec); Mk I* – 2,899ft/sec (884m/sec)

Sights: Blade foresight. Two types of back sight: fixed aperture for up to 900ft (275m); LR lever raised or lowered the rear sight for 900–1,500ft (275–450m). Mk II – rear sights fixed

Range: 1,500ft (450m) effective

Penetration: Subject to target/task

Direct hit at 90°

300ft (91m)	.91in (23mm)
600ft (274m)	.82in (21mm)
1,500ft (457m)	.74in (19mm)

Hit at 40° angle

300ft (91m)	.43in (11mm)
600ft (274m)	.38in (9.6mm)
1,500ft (457m)	.35in (8.8mm).

The first anti-tank rifle, the German T-Gewehr, was a 13mm bolt-action single-shot rifle; the later Russian PTRD-41 went to 14.5mm. The Boys, at .55in, was accurate with good penetration in its day. It could 'kill' the early German PzKpfw I, II and III tanks and all Japanese armour. However, it was heavy, had a huge muzzle blast and signature and a ferocious 'kick' that sullied its reputation. This created a gun-shyness that prompted the Canadians to commission Disney to produce a cartoon to dispel these fears. This

LEFT The Boys anti-tank rifle may seem preposterous today, but in fact it was one of a number of similar such weapons. This is a Mk I* with a bipod (the Mk I had a monopod). In the early war years they proved their worth: in Finland in 1940 they were effective against Soviet BT and T-26 tanks; in Norway they knocked out German PzKpfw Is and IIs; in North Africa they did well against most Italian tanks; and in the Far East they stopped a number of thinly armoured Japanese tanks. *(Simon Clay/Greene Media)*

BELOW A private of the Highland Light Infantry of Canada on a training exercise near Bognor Regis, 7 April 1942. The weapon is a Mk I with a monopod. *(Lt C.E. Nye/Library and Archives Canada PA-211306)*

RIGHT Conceived by Lt Col Stewart Blacker, RA, who also gave the world the Blacker Bombard, the PIAT was developed from Blacker's Baby Bombard by Maj Millis Jefferis. The result was ungainly but effective. *(Simon Clay/Greene Media)*

BELOW This is the equivalent of the big game hunter with his foot on the prize. L/Cpl J.A. Thrasher of the Westminster Regiment, 5th Canadian Armoured Brigade, with the PIAT and the Nashorn 8.8cm self-propelled gun knocked out in Pontecorvo, Italy, on 26 May 1944. *(Lt Strathy E. Smith/ Library and Archives Canada PA-169121)*

cartoon ended by saying '. . . a rifle is like a woman, treat her right and she will never let you down'. It also had too many small parts, making it difficult to service in the field.

All junior ranks were trained in its use – anti-personnel and soft-skinned vehicles as well as armoured – and it was issued one per platoon, carried in the platoon vehicle along with its ammunition. Usually operated by a two-man crew, No 2 carrying ammunition. Accessories included a canvas breech and muzzle cover, cleaning rod, brass loop flannelette pull-through, fine wire gauze for fouling, wire and bristle pull-through brushes and oil.

Projector, Infantry, Anti-Tank (PIAT)

Calibre: 3.3in (83mm)
In service: 1942–50 with British and Commonwealth armies and resistance groups in occupied Europe. Indo-Pakistani War of 1971 and other conflicts worldwide, including Korea

Designed: Maj Millis Jefferis, based on the Blacker Bombard
Manufacturers: ICI (Imperial Chemical Industries) and other state-approved firms
Number produced: 115,000
Weight: 32lb (15kg)
Overall length: 39in (1m)
Barrel length: About a third of weapon length
Ammunition: Shaped/hollow charge which could penetrate almost all enemy armour subject to range – HEAT, HE – supplied in three-round containers; projectile weight 2.5lb (1.1kg)
Feed: Hand-fed/loaded via open trough on the top front of the weapon
Rate of fire: Single shot with a recoil recocking system
Muzzle velocity: 250ft/sec (76m/sec) – generating huge pressure against the shoulder
Penetration: 3–4in (75–100mm) of armour at 90°
Sights: Rear left-mounted aperture. Folding front sight
Range: Realistically 150ft or so for an effective kill. Indirect fire up to 1,050ft (320m).

An effective anti-tank weapon that could also be used for bunker busting and against fortifications, the PIAT had no backblast to give its position away and could penetrate most armour. Although they could be deflected if they didn't hit straight on and side armour (*Schürzen*) could degrade penetration, PIATs accounted for about 7% of German armour in 1944–45.

To reload, the firer stood on the shoulder pad, pulled and turned the tube upwards causing both spring and spigot to engage a seer. This proved difficult for the smaller/ shorter soldier as it meant pulling 200lb (90kg) standing or prone. Trigger-operated, a spigot spring activated the propellant charge.

Ordnance QF 2-pounder

Calibre: 1.575in (40mm)

In service: 1938–45

Variants: In the Second World War the Mk IX was the main production model with an autofrettage barrel (a method of fabrication in which tubing thickness is reduced without compromising the strength of the barrel). The Mk XA was a simplified version of the Mk IX and the Mk XB had a forged barrel

Designed: Vickers, 1936

Manufacturers: Vickers, with a Woolwich (Royal) Arsenal carriage that was easier and cheaper producer

Number produced: 12,000

Weight: 1,848lb (831.6kg); shot weighed 2lb 2oz (1kg)

Length: 6ft 10in (2.08m) excluding carriage

Barrel length: 6ft 7in (2m)

Ammunition: APCR

Elevation: -13° to +15°

Traverse: 360°

Height: 5ft (1.5m) to top of gun shield

Rate of fire: 22 rounds/min

Penetration: AP, hitting armour sloped at 60°, 1.8in (49mm) at 300ft (91.5m)

Muzzle velocity: 2,600ft/sec (792m/sec)

Sights: No 24b, 2× sighting telescope. Iron sight, but the armoured shield had to be lowered

Range: 1,800ft (548m) effective; 3,000ft (914m) max.

Quick-firing, with a stable but heavy carriage, mobile – towed or mounted on vehicles or carriers – with an ammunition box on the gun frame, the 2pdr was obsolete by the beginning of the war in Europe although it performed well in the Far East as the Japanese tanks were lighter and less well-armoured. However, as armour improved it became ineffective. Outranged and lacking an HE shell, it was, however, easier to produce than the improved 6pdr under development and with an invasion of Britain possible, production of the 2pdr continued. They replaced the weapons abandoned to the Germans after the retreat at Dunkirk and would continue in service until the QF 6pdr arrived in 1942. Their lack of hitting power was noticeable in the North African desert – so much so that the 25pdr field gun was used in the anti-tank role.

ABOVE It's easy to forget when discussing the lack of potency of the 2pdr in the North African desert against the German Panzers that in Malaya against Japanese tanks it performed well. In particular, the ambush at Gemensah Bridge during the 14–22 January 1942 Battle of Muar when Sgt Charles Parsons and his crew of 2/4th Anti-tank Regiment knocked out six of the nine Type 95 light tanks the Japanese lost on the 18th. Despite the significant losses – they suffered over 1,000 casualties – the Japanese were able to continue the advance, but not before they had massacred 145 Australians and Indians at Parit Sulong. The photograph shows the height of the 2pdr upon its cruciform mount, from which the wheels had to be removed to fight. Note the 'Bombay Bloomers' worn by the man to the left. These could be folded and buttoned to form shorts.

BELOW The need for mobility in the desert led to the use of portéed guns, the 2pdr being ideal for this role. While the British took a long time to come to terms with the tactics necessary to beat the Germans in the desert, the portée 2pdrs had their moments, one of which was the action at Sidi Rezegh when Lt George Gunn of the 3rd Regiment, RHA, won a posthumous VC. Coincidentally, on the same day, another Old Sedberghian serving with the RHA, Brig 'Jock' Wilson, also won a VC at Sidi Rezegh.

The 2pdr had a semi-automatic vertical-block breech, a hydrospring recoil system with a 20in (50cm) recoil and a three-legged carriage that folded out after removing the wheels. It could be fired with the wheels on, but this limited the traverse. The crew was 3–5 (commander, loader, gunlayer, others as needed for ammunition carriage). In 1938 it was crewed by the Royal Artillery attached to an army division but later in the war the crewing was handed over to the infantry.

Ordnance QF 6-pounder

Calibre: 2.24in (57mm)
In service: 1942–60s
Variants: Gun – British Mk I (development model) had an L/50 (long) barrel and limited production; the Mk II had an L/43 shorter barrel due to a shortage of tooling at that stage of the war (production started in 1941); Mks III and V were designed for tanks; Mk IV had an L/50 (long) barrel with a single-baffled muzzle break. US 57mm Gun M1 and M1A2 Carriage – four British versions (Mks I, IA, II, III, the latter for airborne use) and six US (M1, M1A1, M1A2, M1A3, M2, M2A1)
Designed: Woolwich Arsenal, 1940
Manufacturers: Woolwich (Royal) Arsenal, Australia, Canada, South Africa and over 15,500 by the United States
Number produced: 35,000 of all variants
Weight: 1.25 tons (1,143kg); shot weighed 6.28lb (2.84kg)
Length: Mk II – 8ft 5in (2.44m) excluding

carriage; Mk IV – 9ft 9in (2.56m)
Barrel length: Mk II – 8ft 4in (2.54m)
Ammunition: AP, APCBC (from 1943), HE and, from 1944, the world's first APDS
Elevation: -5° to +15°
Traverse: 90° (45° L and 45° R)
Height: 4ft 2in (1.28m) to top of gun shield (side shields available but rarely used)
Rate of fire: 15 rounds/min
Penetration: At 4,800ft (1,500m) – AP, 2.8in (70mm); APDS, 4.8in (120mm). Against 30° sloped armour at 3,000ft (914m) – AP, 2.9in (74mm); APDS, 5.75in (146mm)
Muzzle velocity: AP – 2,693ft/sec (820m/sec); HE – 2,700ft/sec (880m/sec); APDS – 4,050ft/sec (1,234 m/sec)
Sights: No 24c
Range: 4,950ft (1,510m) effective; 15,000ft (4,600m) max.

The 6pdr breech-loading anti-tank gun fired a variety of ammunition with good long-range penetration. The first gun to 'bag' a Tiger I in 1943 and the first to fire APDS, it was – subject to range – capable of taking on both Tigers and Panthers frontally. Originally controlled by Royal Artillery then passed on to the army in early 1943, the 6pdr had a vertical sliding block, a hydro-pneumatic recoil system and a split-trail carriage. Its crew was 5–6 as circumstances dictated (commander, loader, gunlayer and others as needed for ammunition). It could be towed or used portée – from the back of a vehicle.

Grenades

No 36M grenade

In service: 1915–80s
Variants: Rifle grenade – originally, during the First World War, this was a grenade attached to a metallic rod inserted down the barrel and initiated by a blank cartridge. It was dangerous for the firer and was replaced by a can-shaped holder – the rifle grenade discharger – attached to the muzzle. A gas seal disc was screwed on to the grenade base plug. The grenade was then placed in the cup, the safety pin removed and firing was initiated by a blank cartridge. (Not fired from the shoulder!)

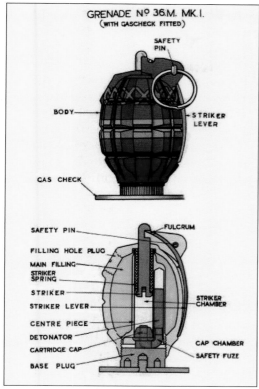

GRENADE Nº 36.M. MK.I.
(WITH GASCHECK FITTED)

SAFETY PIN
BODY
STRIKER LEVER
GAS CHECK

SAFETY PIN
FULCRUM
FILLING HOLE PLUG
MAIN FILLING
STRIKER SPRING
STRIKER
STRIKER LEVER
STRIKER CHAMBER
CENTRE PIECE
DETONATOR
CARTRIDGE CAP
CAP CHAMBER
BASE PLUG
SAFETY FUZE

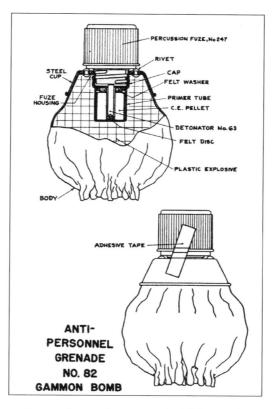

PERCUSSION FUZE, No.247
STEEL CUP
RIVET
CAP
FELT WASHER
FUZE HOUSING
PRIMER TUBE
C.E. PELLET
DETONATOR No.63
FELT DISC
PLASTIC EXPLOSIVE
BODY

ADHESIVE TAPE

ANTI-
PERSONNEL
GRENADE
NO. 82
GAMMON BOMB

FAR LEFT Main features of the No 36M Mk I grenade.

LEFT Main features of the No 82 Gammon bomb.

Designed: William Mills (Sir William from 1922) in 1915, based on a number of earlier designs from abroad
Manufacturers: Mills Munition Factory, Birmingham, and other munitions factories in the UK and Allied countries
Number produced: 75 million from 1915
Weight: 1.7lb (0.45kg)
Fillings: Amatol, Baratol and Trotyl (green band), HE (red markings above the green), sealed and waterproofed for use in the tropics (red crosses)
Range: 75–105ft (20–30m) thrown; 600ft (185m) rifle grenade discharger.

The Mills bomb's classic pineapple casing provided grip for throwing (not to aid fragmentation). It was the first proper fragmentation grenade but used as a defensive weapon thrown from behind cover to wound/kill with an unpredictable pattern of fragmentation. An offensive grenade relies on the shock/blast effect and doesn't fragment. The German Stielhandgranate 24, for example, the 'potato masher', contrary to most war films was a not a fragment but a blast grenade and could be thrown while advancing.

Preparation and use was straightforward:
- unscrew the base plug
- insert a time delay detonator
- rescrew the plug
- take a firm grip around the body and strike lever/spoon
- remove the safety pin by pulling a metal ring with a finger – never teeth because they would break
- throw the grenade overarm or 'slot' it through an aperture. The throw released the strike lever that activated the timed fuse. The initial time delay of 7 seconds was reduced to 4 because it could be thrown back, and sometimes was
- Ideally see where it lands, owing to the blast radius. Preferably from behind cover, because with a blast area of about 300ft (92m) it was potentially lethal to both sides.

No 82 grenade – the Gammon bomb
In service: 1943–45
Designed: Capt R.S. Gammon. He had experience of the No 74 Sticky bomb, which could be (and was) as lethal to the user as it was to the enemy! His design was an improvement

Manufacturers: Contracted UK factories
Number produced: Many thousands
Weight: 12oz (340g) empty; 31.7oz (900g) full
Filling: A plastic (mouldable) explosive, Composition C.

The Gammon bomb had a fabric elasticised bag/body that would be filled depending on the requirement – for example, shrapnel added to the explosive for anti-personnel or all charge for anti-tank purposes. The adaptability of an adjustable charge – the 'do it yourself bomb' – extended to being able to heat rations without smoke.

Hand thrown from behind cover, the cap was unscrewed to expose a weighted tape wrapped around the fuse. When thrown, the momentum released the tape that pulled out a retaining pin, thus arming the grenade. On impact the No 247 'Allways fuze' ensured that the striker hit the percussion cap and detonated the grenade regardless of which part of the grenade hit the target. Impact led to a shockwave with no time delay.

The drawbacks of the Gammon bomb were its poor range and its danger to the user (all stocks were destroyed postwar as they were considered too dangerous).

Other types of British grenade

No 68: The very first hollow-charge weapon in military service. Based on a 2in mortar bomb, the No 68 was not used in any great numbers and was issued to the Home Guard in 1944 when better weapons were available for the troops.

No 69: With a Bakelite shell for blast effect, a metal fragmentation sleeve could be added. Like the Gammon bomb it exploded on impact using the Allways fuze. Its main weaknesses were a small fragmentation area and an all-round blast that could damage the thrower if used in the attack.

No 73: The Thermos bomb was originally a Home Defence anti-tank grenade made from a Thermos-sized bottle filled with TNT. (A smaller version was used in the assassination of Reinhard Heydrich in Prague in 1942.) It also used the Allways fuze.

No 74: The Sticky bomb was a glass sphere filled with nitroglycerine and other additives, covered by an adhesive bandage and finally a spherical sheet-metal casing. It had a 5-second fuse and was a very close-quarter weapon.

GRENADE Nº 69. MK. I.

SAFETY CAP — ADHESIVE TAPE
RING OF RED CROSSES — UPPER BODY
GREEN BAND — LOWER BODY
BASE PLUG

FUZE NO 247 — CLOSING CAP
BALL — SAFETY BOLT WITH SAFETY TAPE AND LEAD WEIGHT
STRIKER — MECHANISM HOLDER
SPRING — HARD RUBBER WASHER GRAPHITED
PELLET CAP — DETONATOR SLEEVE
PERCUSSION CAP — EXPLOSIVE
TUBE — RUBBER PLUG SECURED IN BASE PLUG
DETONATOR NO 46 FILLING HOLE PLUG — BASE PLUG

RIGHT Main features of the No 69 Mk I grenade.

FAR RIGHT Main features of the Sticky bomb.

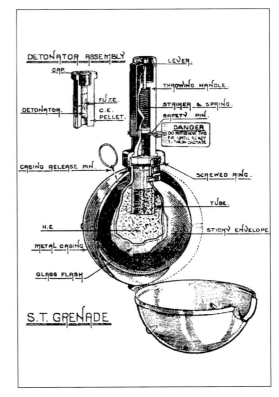

DETONATOR ASSEMBLY
CAP — LEVER.
DETONATOR. — THROWING HANDLE.
FUZE. — STRIKER & SPRING.
C.E. PELLET. — SAFETY PIN.
DANGER DO NOT REMOVE THIS PIN UNTIL READY TO THROW GRENADE.
CASING RELEASE PIN. — SCREWED RING.
H.E — TUBE.
METAL CASING. — STICKY ENVELOPE.
GLASS FLASK.

S.T. GRENADE.

No 75: The Hawkins Grenade was more versatile than the Nos 73 and 74. Pressure-detonated to disable vehicles and tank-tracks, it could also be thrown if fitted with a blasting cap or used for demolitions with cordtex.

Mines

British anti-tank and anti-personnel mines

Variants: AT – Mks II–IV, disabling mines; Mk V, most commonly used and more than capable of dealing with almost all tanks especially when doubled up.

AP – Mks I–II, tripwire-activated with a shrapnel radius of up to 90ft (30m); Mk III – pressure-activated when advancing, causing the mine to spring upward and explode. Radius also 90ft (30m).

Construction: AT – metal body filled with explosive and a pressure plate-activated fuse. Primary purpose to disable a vehicle or destroy it.

AP – variety of construction and sophistication. Primary role to disable personnel and so tie up others to take casualties to the rear. Method of operation mainly pressure or tripwire.

Filling: Most common were TNT and Baratol. AT mines were mainly filled with TNT, Amatol or gelignite.

Markings: Designation, filling and date of manufacture stencilled on body and some with special markings and colour.

Number produced: 18 million+.

Flamethrower

No 2 Mk II Portable Flamethrower

In service: From June 1944
Designed: 1942–43
Number produced: 7,000
Weight: 64lb (29kg)
Range: 90–120ft (30–35m).

Very similar to the German First World War Wechselapparat (Wex) of 1917 and nicknamed the 'Lifebuoy' for its shape, the British portable flamethrower was ready for use by D-Day, although in reality British use of these weapons was much more centred around the Wasp (Universal Carrier conversion) or Crocodile (Churchill tank). The doughnut-shaped backpack fuel container (capacity 4gal/18 litres) was considered the best shape to contain fuel under high pressure. In the middle of the 'doughnut' was a container holding nitrogen gas under pressure (140bar) to propel the burning fuel. Ignition was by cartridges in the nozzle: some held up to ten, which allowed the operator ten 1-second bursts or he could spray fuel and then ignite it.

It was a heavy and an unreliable weapon: if the battery got wet it wouldn't function. A lighter – 48lb (22kg) rather than 64lb (29kg) – version, nicknamed the Ack-Ack, would have been used against Japan had the war not ended.

ABOVE LEFT AND ABOVE Throwing a grenade. The British had been taught from the First World War to lob the grenade to clear cover and obstructions. In 1940 they found the seven-second fuse too long. Shortened to four seconds, grenades were delivered by whatever means suited the tactical situation – including 'posting' into bunkers or through windows.

LEFT Initially, the portable flamethrower could manage ten 1-second bursts at short range (30–40 yd) so operators needed to be able to use it carefully. Here a corporal from the Dutch Prinses Irene Brigade practises firing a lifebuoy flamethrower. *(Nationaalarchief.nl)*

BELOW Motorised flamethrowers – the Crocodile tanks and Wasp Universal Carriers – were used more frequently by British forces than the one-man variety. Developed by both British and Canadians (who produced their own first version, the Ronson and went on to convert turretless Ram tanks into flamethrowers), the Wasp came in three versions: the Mk I (thrower fixed at front with 100gal tank), Mk II (flamethrower in co-driver's position) and Mk II* or IIC (Canadian version with fuel tanks on rear of vehicle). This is a IIC.

GUNS

ABOVE The Ordnance QF 25pdr was ubiquitous in British and Commonwealth armies, being found in the field artillery and anti-tank role, towed by Quads (built by various companies) and other methods. It was often used with a trailer/limber which carried 32 rounds of ammunition and, as seen here, the circular firing platform which, once the gun was placed on it, allowed easy 360° traverse.

ABOVE RIGHT A well-known photograph from Juno Beach, the Polsten 20mm cannon (here seen in triple form on a trailer) was the result of a Polish design team who escaped their country in 1939 and RSAF Enfield. A cheaper version of the Oerlikon cannon, it saw service with AA platoons of 21st Army Group in 1944–45, the Canadian John Inglis & Co. providing the mounts. *(Library and Archives Canada)*

CENTRE The Bofors 20mm AA gun was widely used by the Allies as a light AA gun. In British use it had a complicated Kerrison Predictor but was usually used with the Stiffkey sight. The Bofors were also used against ground targets: this battery is firing at German targets over the Rhine.

RIGHT Airborne and mountain troops require lighter, more mobile equipment and this was particularly true when it came to artillery. The QF 3.7in mountain gun was used throughout the war and some 825 of the American 75mm M1 pack howitzer (often referred to by its 1960s M116 designation) – as seen here in use at Arnhem – were provided under Lend-Lease and saw use by mountain and airlanding (glider-borne) units.

Chapter Six

Transport and communications

The British Army was fully
motorised, with vehicles from
a range of sources in Britain
and North America. Having lost
so many in 1940 they had to
procure vehicles quickly. They
did so initially by requisitioning
from private sources but also
by making use of the powerful
industrial capability of Canada,
which would go on to build more
lorries than any other country.

**OPPOSITE It could be 1944 in this scene showing a 'Katy'
(Austin K2/Y) ambulance and Bedford OYD '3-tonner' outside
an aircraft hangar.** *(Alec Small)*

RIGHT There are some places that only animal transport will reach. SEAC had on strength in April 1945 no fewer than 23,595 mules, 6,758 horses and 739 donkeys. This mule's load was a 3in mortar tripod and various boxes. Note the mule's fringed headband, helpful to keep flies at bay.

BELOW The Canadian Military Pattern (CMP) series of trucks and lorries (more than 90 vehicles with countless body types) provided over half a million vehicles to British, Commonwealth and many other countries during the war. Chassis were mostly built by General Motors of Canada Ltd as well as Ford and Chrysler Canada. Bodies were produced by a range of manufacturers. It's a great claim to fame that Canada's wartime production was larger than that of all the Axis powers put together. Here, a convoy of Chevrolet CMP trucks crosses a temporary bridge near Phyu on the way to Rangoon.

Transport

All manner of vehicles were used by British and Commonwealth infantrymen during the Second World War. This situation came about for many reasons, not the least of which was the amount of materiel left behind after the Dunkirk evacuation in May and June 1940, when some 75,000 vehicles were abandoned. To a large extent, the War Ministry simply had little choice but to obtain replacements wherever it could. The British Army therefore requisitioned more or less every civilian vehicle it could find to help make up the deficiency. Although the massive losses sustained almost broke the nation, it must be remembered that a huge amount of it was incredibly out-of-date equipment that was left over from the First World War. Had it not been lost, the penny-pinching politicians of the day would have forced our troops to use it to counter the vastly superior Nazi materiel that was ranged against them, with predictable results. As it was, the replacements – when they eventually came – were generally either up to the job or in some cases even very good.

RIGHT The Morris Commercial C8 was the basis for the famous Quad FAT. It also came in a 4 × 4 GS utility vehicle (as here). It was introduced in 1944 and other models included radio, office, air compressor and water-tank versions. The cargo truck could be found with either wood or steel body. Note the yellow disc with black numeral 5 indicating bridging classification. These figures were made up from information about the vehicles including loaded and unloaded weights, number and spacing of axles, vehicle speed and so on. The most common bridging plate numbers are shown in the box. *(Rob Mitchell/WikiCommons (CC0))*

The typical infantryman would have encountered many different kinds of transportation, but broadly, these can be divided into the following categories:

- **Trucks and lorries** – the workhorses of every military operation, these were used to transport the vast quantities of supplies needed to keep an army going, from taking arms and ammunition up to the front line to

BRITISH BRIDGE PLATES

Class	Vehicles
1	Motorcycles (with or without sidecars), small 2–3 seat saloon cars, jeeps, 10cwt two-wheeled trailers
2	Jeeps, 2–7 seat saloon cars, light utilities (*eg* Humber Snipe), 8cwt truck, most 15cwt two-wheeled trailers
3	Bren carriers, heavy saloon cars, some 15cwt trucks, some 2-ton four-wheeled trailers
4	Daimler Dingo and Humber Mk 1 scout cars 15cwt GS truck, most Universal Carriers
5	Most 15cwt trucks, including C15A, Morris C8 portée, Ford Lynx, White M3A1, Windsor Universal Carriers
6	Most 30cwt 4 × 4 lorries, Quads, 5-ton four-wheeled radar trailers
7	Some 3-ton 4 × 2 lorries, 40mm Bofors, Daimler and Humber armoured cars
8	Some 3-ton trucks, M14 GMC and 5-ton four-wheeled GS trailers
9	Probably the biggest category with some 4×2 3-tonners, the majority of 3-ton 6×4 and 6×6 trucks, Caterpillar D9 tractors, 5-ton four-wheeled laundry trailers, DUKWs
10	Thornycroft WZ/TC4 tippers, 7-ton lorries, six-wheeled recovery trailers
11	Diamond T 4-ton 6 × 6, pontoon carriers and wreckers
12	AEC Matador, AEC ACV, Leyland retriever 3-ton 6 × 4 machinery lorries, Diamond T 6 × 6 crane, Mack LMSW 5-ton 6 × 6 heavy breakdown trucks
15	Stuart tanks, Staghound armoured cars
16	Valentine tank
17	Mack NM6 6-ton 6 × 4 and White 6 × 6 GS trucks
18	Diamond T M20 12-ton tractors, Valentine bridgelayers
21	Mack NR9 10-ton 6 × 4 and NM3 10-ton GS trucks
24	Matilda tank, Caterpillar D8 tractors
30	Cromwell tank, Ram II APC, Sexton 25pdr SP guns
33	M10, Sherman tanks
40	Churchill tank

evacuating the wounded back to safer areas. The difference between how the British Army classified these vehicles was that a truck was considered to have a payload capacity of 1 ton or less, whereas a lorry could take 30cwt (1.5 tons) or more. This was further refined in that a van was a truck with a box roof, and a tractor was a lorry that was primarily intended to pull or tow something; this is why the vehicles that towed artillery guns were designated as tractors. Example manufacturers include AEC, Bedford, Austin and Leyland.

■ **Artillery tractors** – infantry units usually had their own embedded artillery, and so while these vehicles were not actually used by riflemen, they would have been part of the everyday scenery. Whereas prewar it had been standard practice to use tracked towing vehicles known as 'Dragons', for reasons of cost and performance, these had more or less all been replaced by 1940. From then on, field guns were typically towed by 1.5-ton Morris 'Quads' or their equivalent, while medium artillery was moved using 3-ton six-wheeled Scammells. Example manufacturers include Guy, Morris and Scammell.

■ **Armoured personnel carriers** – these were used to carry soldiers, providing light protection against rifle and machine-gun fire. They allowed the troops to stay close to the front line even when it was fast-moving. Example manufacturers include Vickers-Armstrong and Vivian Loyd & Co.

■ **Armoured cars** – these were mostly operated by reconnaissance units or by officers wanting to stay close to the action. Example manufacturers include Daimler and Humber.

■ **Cars** – a wide variety of these were used, such as those utilised by couriers or officers, with the jeep being by far the best known. Example manufacturers include Rover, Humber, Austin, Ford and Willys.

■ **Motorcycles** – these provided a combination of qualities which made them indispensable to an army where communications were still relatively primitive. They ranged from the robust versions used by the military police and couriers to the folding air-portable lightweights issued to the paratroops. Example manufacturers include Norton, BSA, Matchless and Royal Enfield.

■ **Tanks** – although these would have been a common sight to the infantryman, they were very much the preserve of the armoured columns. Example manufacturers include Vickers-Armstrong, Leyland and Vauxhall.

By mid-war, it had become British Army policy to ensure that all relevant wheeled vehicles had an anti-aircraft sentry who could see through 360° to watch out for enemy attack. While it was possible to engineer this into new designs, existing vehicles were typically modified to make it possible; often this involved cutting round holes in the roofs, although in some instances they simply removed the tops of the cabs. In smaller vehicles, the lookouts would stand on the passenger seat to see, whereas on the larger cargo trucks, the sentry would sit out in the open above the cab.

Many of the above vehicles were also able to tow trailers, of which there were a huge number of different varieties. It is hard to emphasise just how important they were. Examples include:

Trailer 10cwt 2-wheeled Lightweight GS: This was a British-made half-ton trailer – the basic version was intended to be towed by a jeep, but there were two further variants, both of which were similar units that were designed to go behind 15cwt trucks.

Trailer 15cwt 2-wheeled Water 180gal: This was a trailer on to which a 180gal water tank was mounted, as well as all the necessary pumps, filters and hoses for collecting water from streams and then rendering it safe for use by thirsty troops.

Trailer 2-wheeled 22kW Generating Set: This carried a Lister diesel-powered generator to provide electricity for everything from headquarters to radar units to bakeries.

One of the stark differences between British and American vehicles and the consequent rules of the road was that the former used right-hand drive and drove on the left, whereas it was the exact opposite for the latter. While this may seem obvious, the authorities felt it was important enough a matter to highlight in the various British and American army handbooks.

Carriers

Universal Carrier

RIGHT How many men can ride on a carrier? At least ten plus driver, it would appear, if this photograph of a 2nd (BR) Infantry Division unit taken in Burma is anything to go by. The Universal Carrier or Bren Gun Carrier, introduced in 1940, was a light tracked armoured vehicle that provided the transport mainstay for many infantry units. Manufactured by several different companies, there were a wide variety of variants to cope with the different roles required, including its use as a 2in mortar or MMG carrier or with a flamethrower.

Loyd Carrier

RIGHT A 49th (West Riding) Division Loyd Carrier towing a 6pdr anti-tank gun (its primary function) and transporting its crew, alongside a knocked-out Panther during Operation Epsom, 27 June 1944. Although the Loyd Carrier isn't as well known as the Universal Carrier, it was still a mainstay of the British and Commonwealth forces, with some 26,000 being produced for the war effort by Loyd, Ford, Wolseley, Dennis, Aveling & Barford and Sentinel. There were several types made, including: Tracked Personnel Carrier used to transport troops; Tracked Towing to tow a 4.2in mortar or an anti-tank gun; Tracked Starting and Charging for armoured regiments; and Tracked Cable Layer Mechanical supplied to the Royal Corps of Signals in order to lay communications lines more quickly.

Windsor Carrier

RIGHT From the Windsor Carrier technical manual, this photograph shows the canvas tent provided for all-weather crew protection. The Windsor was a lengthened – by 28in (72cm) – Canadian-built variant of the Universal Carrier. Over 25,000 Universal Carriers were manufactured in Canada, and 5,000 Windsors. (*Cobbaton Combat Collection*)

AFVs

Ram Kangaroo APC

RIGHT The development of the APC took place in Normandy in 1944. The brainchild of Canadian Lt Gen Guy Simonds, the first 'Defrocked Priests' were M7 Priests with their 105mm howitzer removed by the REME. This worked so well in Operation Totalize that the idea was pursued and the 1st Canadian Armoured Personnel Carrier Squadron was created.

BELOW The Ram Kangaroo was the APC version of the Canadian Ram tank, creating the first mechanised infantry units. This one, at Mill in the Netherlands, commemorates the 1st Canadian Armoured Carrier Regiment, a title conferred on 1 January 1945. Previously, two units had been created: the 1st Canadian and the British 49th Armoured Personnel Carrier Regiments under 79th Armoured Division.

BELOW The US Army's M3 halftrack was also used extensively, although this was only lightly armoured (unlike the Ram's tank hull). The Lend-Lease version was designated M5.

CT15A Armoured Truck

BELOW The CT15A armoured truck was a multi-purpose vehicle marrying the chassis of the Chevrolet C15 CMP truck with an armoured hull made by Hamilton Bridge. It could be used as an APC, ambulance or load-shifter. *(Lt Barney J. Gloster/Library and Archives Canada PA-115394)*

Morris C8 Quad Field Artillery Tractor

BELOW Quad Morris C8 FAT towing a 25pdr and its limber. A number of companies built Quad FATs, including Chevrolet and Ford, based on the CMP chassis.

Trucks and lorries

Bedford MW General Service Truck

RIGHT A successful design, the Bedford MW was used in many roles both by infantry and other units. The MWG was the version that carried a portée 2pdr anti-tank or Oerlikon 20mm AA gun (among other weapons). Although it was only two-wheel drive, it was good enough to remain in service until the late 1950s and more than 66,000 were built in total. *(Alec Small)*

Bedford OY Lorry

RIGHT This beautifully restored OYD shows off the classic 3-tonner – built in greater numbers than any other equivalent British wartime lorry. The short wheelbase version was the OX. *(Alec Small)*

Bicycles

LEFT There are many D-Day photos of soldiers making their way down the gangways of landing ships with bicycles. One company in each of D-Day's follow-up battalions were to use them. In fact, most troops didn't and many of the bikes – to the delight of the locals – were quickly abandoned. The BSA folding bike, originally developed for use by Airborne troops, was the main type used. *(Alec Small)*

Military cars

Military cars came from two main sources, either as requisitioned civilian vehicles or those built for the armed forces from standard production models. As a result of the wartime shortage of more or less everything, there was little choice but to use whatever was available. Consequently, there were many different makes and models in use, including those produced by Humber (Snipe or Super Snipe), Austin (Models 8 and 10), Vauxhall (J-type and H-type), Hillman (Minx) and Ford (WOA1 and WOA2). When the Lend-Lease system came into being, the ground-breaking Willys Jeep was shipped across the Atlantic by the thousands. This transformed the lives of untold numbers of soldiers who until then had largely to rely on carriers and trucks to cross long distances.

All the above can be broadly categorised as either a staff car, a utility or a tourer. Some models – such as the Ford WOA1/WOA2 – were supplied in all three formats. Those designated as Staff Cars had to be able to carry at least four men together with all their equipment, including their personal weapons. As they were intended for use on the road,

ABOVE General Montgomery's staff car (M 239485) was based on the chassis of the prewar Humber Super Snipe with bodywork by Thrupp & Maberly. It featured a canvas folding roof, larger and wider wings accommodate larger and wider wheels and military pattern tyres. Note the general's red star plate with four gold stars – these would increase to five when he was promoted to field marshal – and the flag on the bonnet front which was flown when he was in the car (which was a lot: he covered 60,000 miles in six months in north-west Europe). *(Alf van Beem/WikiCommons (CC0))*

Humber 'Box' Heavy Utility FWD

BELOW Humber's prewar civilian luxury limos, the Snipe and Super Snipe, were much used as staff cars but the army needed an FWD to give all-terrain capability. The 'Box' was an excellent solution. Even larger than the WOA2, it could accommodate senior officers, staff (it had two armchair seats and two smaller dickie seats could be erected behind) and maps/equipment etc. The four back seats could easily be demounted to provide a comfortable sleeping area. The 'Box' proved an excellent vehicle for commanders in the field, and were – for example – used by brigadiers in command of an infantry brigade. *(Alec Small)*

Willys Jeep

BELOW Well over 640,000 jeeps were built during the war, including over 360,000 Willys MBs and 270,000 Ford GPs. With its powerful engine, light weight, rugged construction and four-wheel drive capability, it could go almost anywhere. President Eisenhower considered it to be one of the three most decisive Allied weapons of the war.

they did not need four-wheel drive, especially high ground clearances or cross-country tyres. They did, however, need to be able to cope with rough tracks, and so had to be built to a robust standard. The main priority beyond the above was that they also needed to provide enough room to enable maps to be spread out so that officers concerned could work together on the move.

Wartime blackout regulations also covered cars, and so all had special covers fitted to reduce light output to a minimum; unsurprisingly, this led to a lot of unnecessary accidents.

Motorcycles

Motorcycles were an essential part of the way the British and Commonwealth armies functioned, and this was recognised in standing regulations which detailed that all officers below the rank of colonel had to be proficient on a motorcycle. This was primarily so that when things got really snarled up at the front, an officer could navigate his way through the traffic and get to where he needed to be. An extreme example of this was when, during the evacuation of Dunkirk, they were used by officers – right in the face of the enemy — to find British stragglers and then to help them navigate back to the disembarkation points. Many were killed, injured or taken prisoner on such duties.

Where more day-to-day activities were concerned, motorcycles were used primarily for dispatch work, as convoy escorts and for reconnaissance activities. They were often used to convey messages that were too sensitive to be transmitted by radio or via telegraph wires in case they were intercepted by the enemy. It was, after all, standard practice for German signals troops to tap into British communications lines whenever they could. In other instances, they cut the lines, so in many situations it was safer to send a dedicated messenger on a motorcycle.

Being a dispatch rider involved all manner of hazards as they were seen by the enemy as being important targets. Consequently they were often the focus of snipers, fighter planes and ground troops. As the war went on and the fighting got dirtier, they also had to face wires stretched taut across roads and tracks.

James ML 'Military Lightweight'

ABOVE The James ML was a rudimentary motorcycle that was designed to be air-portable. As such, it had a small 125cc two-stroke motor, hand gear-change and an abbreviated exhaust. Here it is modelled by Brigade Sgt Maj R.M. Cooper of the 9th Canadian Infantry Brigade, Carpiquet, 12 July 1944. *(Lt Ken Bell/Library and Archives Canada PA-162538)*

Harley-Davidson WL

BELOW The Harley-Davidson WL was available in various different formats. Being American-made, Harley-Davidsons were rarely used by British forces but 20,000 of the WLC version (seen here) were issued to the Canadian forces. *(Library and Archives Canada PA-064510)*

Many an unwary or tired rider literally had his head cut off by such means. On top of all this were the perennial risks of riding a motorcycle, namely poor roads, other road users, bad weather and machine breakdowns.

In order to minimise the risks of becoming a target, all riders had to use headlights fitted with special masks that reduced the light output to a minimum. This alone caused countless accidents where hazards like potholes, shell-holes or fallen trees could not be seen before it was too late.

Although a lot of different makes and models of motorcycle saw service with British and Commonwealth forces during the Second World War, all needed to be looked after properly with regular routine maintenance. On a daily basis this would involve such things as checking the tyres for damage and correct inflation, that the drive chain was receiving the required lubrication, that cable-operated controls were functioning properly, that the engine, chaincase and transmission oils were at the optimum levels and so on. Depending on the model and the use the machine had been under, other things like the clutch and the magneto contact breakers may also have needed to be cleaned and/or adjusted. Riders were not expected to do much more than this – any really serious work was undertaken by army mechanics.

WELBIKE

Manufacturers: Excelsior Motor Company
Engine: 98cc, air-cooled two-stroke single
Top speed: 30mph (48km/h)
Transmission: Single-speed; chain final drive
Suspension: None
Brakes: Drum rear
Weight: 71lb (32kg) dry
Fuel capacity: 0.81gal (3.7 litres)

The Welbike was a super-lightweight motorcycle expressly designed to be folded down and air-dropped inside a standard parachute container – a CLE Canister. To this end, there was no room for luxuries like suspension, a front brake and lights. Initially, it was for use by the Special Operations Executive; however, it was also issued to paratroopers of the British 1st and 6th Airborne Divisions at Arnhem as part of Operation Market Garden. Powered by a tiny 98cc Villiers two-stroke engine, the light overall weight

meant that it returned excellent fuel consumption – despite having a small fuel tank, it still had a useful range of about 90 miles (145km) when travelling at 30mph (48km/h). On extraction from the delivery container – specially marked with the words 'Motor Cycle', assembly for use was incredibly fast – if all went well, it could be ridden in just over 10 seconds. Only three operations were required – the handlebars needed to be twisted into position and locked, then the seat was pulled up (in the manner of a bicycle), and the footrests folded out; the engine was push-started.

Although they were initially only issued to airborne troops, before long they were also being used by ground forces, such as those who landed at Anzio and Normandy. Three versions of the Welbike were produced, with a total of over 3,600 being manufactured.

Although the basic idea of the Welbike was a good one, the reality was that many were abandoned on the battlefield either because their containers landed too far from the troops (being heavier, they dropped differently), or because their small wheels were unable to cope with rough terrain. To an extent, they were also superseded by bigger machines when larger military gliders became available.

LEFT Making airborne troops more mobile was a good idea and one that was answered in a number of ways: folding bicycles – such as the BSA airborne bicycle – and the miniature Welbike were both excellent ideas overtaken by events. Gliders allowed jeeps and larger motorcycles better suited to rough terrain to be used. Ironically, as pointed out on www.oldbike.eu, when British airborne troops did utilise bicycles in great numbers in the hurried advance to Wismar in 1945, as the Allies thrust to the Baltic, they had to use captured bicycles! *(Royal Signals Museum)*

Norton 16H

ABOVE Norton produced around 100,000 motorcycles for the military during the war. By far the majority were the 500cc single-cylinder side-valve four-stroke 16H that was used as a general workhorse. The Norton 16H was used extensively by the military police for all manner of organisational and security matters. Here L/Cpl Don Fife of No 2 Provost Company, Canadian Provost Corps, pauses to check his map while en route to Falaise at Fresney-le-Puceau, **12 August 1944.** *(Lt Michael M. Dean/Library and Archives Canada PA-169324)*

Matchless

ABOVE The Matchless was one of some 80,000 used by British and Commonwealth troops. Sitting on it is Lt G. Murray Williams of Headquarters Company, 1st Canadian Parachute Battalion, advancing from Lembeck through Coesfeld, Germany, 30 March 1945. *(Lt Charles H. Richer/Library and Archives Canada PA-206876)*

BELOW British infantry were involved in a number of amphibious landings during the war – from Dieppe (mainly Canadians) to the attack on Walcheren during the clearing of the Scheldt and the Rhine crossing in 1945. The major landings – those that involved attack from the sea – saw two main types of equipment used: assault landing craft, whose bows dropped down to allow the soldiers to exit, and the larger LCIs that came in once the landing beaches had been cleared of the enemy. The photograph on the left shows men of 50th (Northumbrian) Division wading ashore from an LSI(L) on one of the Gold Beaches. A swamped Sexton SP gun of 147th Field Regiment (Essex Yeomanry), 56th Infantry Brigade, is visible on the left. Later in the war, particularly for river crossings or in flooded areas, Alligator amphibious vehicles were used. The right-hand photo shows men of the Canadian North Shore Regiment during **Operation Veritable, 8 February 1945.** *(Capt Colin C. McDougall/Library and Archives Canada PA-145769)*

Communications

Signals were crucial to the infantryman of the Second World War, allowing them to work closely with aircraft, artillery and armour, as well as intercommunication within their own units.

'A piece of paper makes you an officer, a radio makes you a commander': General Omar N. Bradley was quoting one of his communications officers when he wrote this in his autobiography, but it sums up well the importance of signals. In the British Army most signals are handled by the Royal Corps of Signals. On 28 June 1920 a royal warrant was signed by the Secretary of State for War (Winston Churchill) giving the sovereign's approval for the creation of the corps. Developed from the RE Signal Service that served during the First World War, its main functions were to provide:

- Technical advice to commanders and staffs at all levels
- Communications down to the point where they were taken over by regimental signallers
- Advice on all signal matters and the training of regimental signalling instructors
- Land communications for the RN and RAF (who undertook to provide some of the personnel for manning the circuits)
- First-line maintenance of signal equipment through the army
- The distribution of certain controlled and project stores in the field in conjunction with the RAOC
- Telecommunication intelligence
- Frequency allotment
- Liaison with the GPO and the post and telegraph departments of allied countries.

From 1943, as a result of the Godwin-Austen Committee, the corps took over the responsibility of signal security and codes and ciphers from the General Staff.

Both these functions were vital to the Allied cause, particularly with wireless communications – lax radio procedure, as was so well shown in the desert, could provide enemy listeners with valuable information. As its responsibilities grew and the war went on, so the number of signallers increased:

RIGHT AND FAR RIGHT The standard infantry short-range radio, the No 38 wireless set was also used to communicate with supporting tanks. The wartime shot is of a No 38 set operator in Apeldoorn. Our reenactor is almost identically equipped: note the long webbing sheath for the antenna.

WARTIME INCREASE OF ROYAL SIGNALS' PERSONNEL

Theatre	Offrs	ORs	Total
BEF 1940	413	12,894	13,307
Middle East 1942	1,135	23,434	24,569
BLA 1945	1,716	34,975	36,691
CMF 1945	1,522	31,132	32,654
India–Burma 1945	2,520	17,601	20,121 (not incl. Indian Signal Corps)
Total signallers worldwide 1945	8,518	142,472	150,990

Communications during the First World War were primarily provided by wire. However, the Battle of Amiens in 1918 proved how successful wireless could be and soon it was apparent that wireless was important from the lowest level. Artillery aerial spotting, of course, needed it, but the Desert War saw the demand for wireless communications increase for all services. The proportion of wireless to line varied in different theatres. In Italy and Sicily the hilly terrain saw telephone and teleprinter circuits often preferred to wireless. In the thick jungles of Burma and New Guinea effective range of wireless equipment was greatly reduced: difficult if not impossible. The problems here were mainly caused by moisture as signallers found that flat, damp jungle was worse than dry, hilly conditions. Indeed, as well as this, fewer frequencies were workable at night in the jungle than in other theatres. In Burma, confidence in wireless communication was also undermined by lack of spare parts and facilities for quick repairs, even after the introduction of new equipment. Col T.B. Gravely gives examples of wire usage during the war:

- *A 4-wire route had to be constructed from Silchar to Imphal, a distance of 125 miles over eight mountain ranges. The track that was followed had to be widened to take jeeps and included 1,200 double hairpin bends; there was seldom less than a 60ft sheer drop on one side. Five Construction Sections completed the route in 4.5 months moving the whole of the stores up in jeeps.*
- *Between El Alamein and Tripoli the Eighth Army put up 600 tons of copper wire. When the route was finished it was possible to speak from Tripoli to Baghdad a distance of over 2,000 miles.*

- *During September and October 1944 the Allied Forces Long Line Control in Paris allotted to the Allied Forces 3,076 circuits representing 205,845 circuit miles, the bulk of them being on rehabilitated routes. It is estimated that up to October 1944 the Allies had constructed 5,000 miles of open wire route, representing 100,000 circuit miles.*
- *In Italy 2,997 miles of underground cable were repaired and taken into service. In addition, 5,635 miles of open wire were in use, about 80 percent of these circuits being on long-distance routes.*

The trouble with line, however, is not just the manpower and time needed to lay it and the problem of damage, but the shipping space required when sent overseas. Operating line is straightforward, as is training, but maintenance is tricky. A sensible mix of options was the answer, as shown by the wartime statistics. Equipment issued 1939–45 included:

- ■ field telephones 631,000
- ■ teleprinters 11,000 (only 181 in use before 1939)
- ■ wireless sets including transmitters 552,500.

Teleprinters were, in effect, typewriters that sent signals either down phone cables or by radio. One thing that lessened as the war went on was the use of motorcycles by the RSigs dispatch service. Dispatch riders were an important adjunct to wire and wireless and their main form of transport in 1939 – various types of motorcycle (see pages 141–143) – worked well when there were decent roads or dry conditions. Unfortunately, there weren't in most locations: desert, mud, flood and icy winter conditions all militated against two-wheel transport. Nevertheless, signals had to keep up with leading troops and it soon became obvious that they had to have the same transport as the units they accompanied, and had to be able to handle a wide range of vehicles including animal packs in difficult country. As air transport became more available, so the jeep and trailer – the largest vehicles easily accommodated – became the vehicles of choice and this meant a reorganisation of loads from those supplied by lorries. Technical vehicles came of age during the war, sometimes with locally designed bodies, although that made replacement difficult.

Unit-level communications

The Royal Signals provided communication services in the field down to the headquarters of regiments. Below this level, unit signallers were responsible for maintaining unit communications with HQs, with units at the same level and supporting artillery. Tank/infantry wireless communication was the responsibility of the tank commander but local communication could be effected thanks to external telephones that were, as the war progressed, placed in an armoured box at the rear of the vehicle (with a long lead on a spring-loaded reel in case the infantryman needed to leave quickly).

The Infantry Division Signal Regiment was first created in 1912 as a company of about 175 all ranks under a major. By 1918 the strength had risen to 415, by 1938 to 491, 1941 to 516, 1943 to 710 and by 1945 to 743. Its main task was to provide the commander and his staff with the communications they needed to fight and to maintain the division, and to supervise and integrate the communications operated with other arms. The CRSigs of the division was technical adviser to the Divisional CO.

Radio equipment saw significant improvement during the war, and by 1945 there were few areas that did not see development. British Army sets were numbered based on a system devised in 1929 but modified slightly over time (see accompanying table). Canadian sets were placed within the same system but there were some from other sources that fell outside.

British Army radio numbering system		
Set No	Range	Purpose
1	Short	Link between brigade and battalion
2	Short	Link between division and brigade
3	Medium	Link between corps and division
4	Medium/long	Link between GHQ and corps
5	Long	Link between base and GHQ
6	Worldwide range	Army chain
7	Special types (originally for AFVs)	
8	Short	Infantry manpack
9	Medium	AFV set
10	Medium	Microwave set

Later sets followed a similar approach to numbering, so the No 9 set was followed by the 19 and so on. During the Second World War most of the sets were not transceivers but required transmitter and receiver units. All these sets also required aerials that came in various forms and lengths. For example, the No 18 manpack set had a Morse range of 2–6 miles (Morse) reduced to 1–3 miles using voice. This was increased when using a 6ft rod aerial to 4–10 miles (Morse) and 2–5 miles (voice). Finally, an 11ft rod aerial improved range to 10 miles (Morse) and 5 miles using voice.

BELOW Layout of the individual elements of the No 38 set.

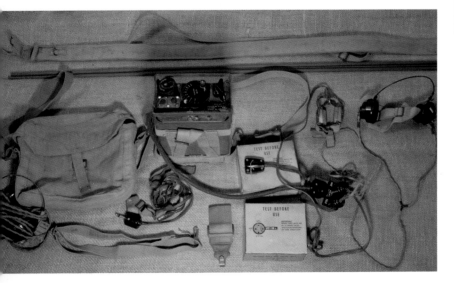

BRITISH SECOND WORLD WAR WIRELESS SETS

No	Date	Main function	Range (miles)	Replaced by
8	1940	Manpack transmitter/receiver for short-range communication in Coy and Bn HQ	5	No 18 set
9	1939	Mobile transmitter/receiver; medium-range vehicle and ground station used for AFVs and divisional signals	35	
9 Mk I Cdn	1943	Canadian transmitter/receiver improved GP version of British No 9 set; could be dismounted and used as a ground station	50	No 52 set
10	1944	Mobile LoC microwave radio relay system providing eight two-way telephone channels; two parabolic aerials, one for receiving, one transmitting	50 (theory; 20 usually)	
11	1938	Portable transceiver; GP low power set. Used as a vehicle, ground and animal pack station	20	Nos 19 and 22 sets
12	1941	Static or vehicle-mounted transmitter station for LoC; usually associated with Reception Set R107 High-power version	60 200 (moving), 1,500 stationary	No 53 set
17	1941	Portable transceiver; main use for searchlight control; also used by AA batteries and RE detachments.	15	
18 Mk III	1940	Manpack transmitter/receiver; short-range communication in forward areas between Bn HQ and Coy HQ RA FOO used the No 18 to communicate with his infantry unit	5	Nos 48/58/ 68 sets (alternatives)

1 The No 8 Set only saw limited production and was replaced by the No 18.
2 The No 11 Set was an excellent prewar design replacing the No 1 Set. It was used for communication with both land and air assets. It was replaced by the No 19 Set.
3 The No 12 Set was usually used with the R107 Reception Set as here. Note the insignia – the Royal Signals shoulder flash, the cross swords of British Army, the signals arm of service colours (see p. 96) and sergeant's stripes.
4 The No 18 Set – receiver at the top and sender below – was the standard British infantry set. The Mk I entered service in 1940 and was quickly produced as the much improved Mk III.
(All pics Royal Signals Museum)

No	Date	Main function	Range (miles)	Replaced by
19 Mk II	1942	Standard Second World War tank set; later used as a GP set. The A set was HF transmitter/receiver for voice and Morse B set VHF voice transceiver; C set was a crew intercom. An added amplifier increased range	15(A)/0.75(B)	
21	1940	Portable transmitter/receiver; used for Inf Bde and RA Regt communication, later employed as GP	5	
22	1942	GP low-power vehicle and ground station with facilities for manpack. Used by AB and AA units	20	No 62 set
26	1944	Multichannel telephone system over VHF link.	40–60	
33	1941	LoC and GP mobile medium transmitter, reworking of No 12 set. Used with R106/R107 reception sets	80	
37	1941	Short-range lightweight transmitter/receiver for use by paras. Some components used in S-Phone	1(ground); 15 (ground to air)	
38 Mk I	1942	Manpack set, also produced as an AFV version for direct communication with infantry	1	No 38 Mk II
38 Mk II	1942	Short-range infantry manpack radio	1	
38 Mk III	1944–45	Tropicalised version of the Mk II	1	
46	1942	Waterproof manpack transceiver, used by beach-landing troops	10	
48	1942	US-made version of No 18 set. Manpack transmitter/receiver.	10	
52	1943	Canadian replacement for No 9 set. Mobile transmitter/receiver; used for communications from Bde to Div	100	
53	1944	Canadian-made mobile medium power transmitter primarily for ACVs and for ground stations	500 (Morse); 100 (voice)	
58	1943	Canadian-made manpack transmitter/receiver alternative to No 18 set; comms between Bn HQ and Coy HQ	5	
62	1945	Portable/mobile transceiver; short-range vehicle-mounted or manpack or animal	25	
68	1943	Similar to No. 18 set, lower frequency range; manpack transmitter/receiver	10	
76	1943	Transmitter set used in conjunction with receiver R109	300	

(Source: Wireless for the Warrior: http://www.wftw.nl/wsets.html)

5

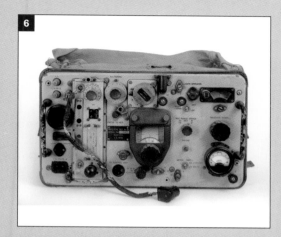

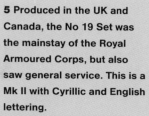

5 Produced in the UK and Canada, the No 19 Set was the mainstay of the Royal Armoured Corps, but also saw general service. This is a Mk II with Cyrillic and English lettering.

6 The No 21 set was a No 11 Set replacement.

7 The No 46 Set was a waterproof manpack set used for amphibious landings.

8 The No 48 Set Mk I was a US development of a similar style as the No 18.

9 This No 53 Set is seen in a command vehicle. It, too, was used in conjunction with the R107 Reception Set.

10 This is a Canadian No 58 Mk I Set, a version of the No 18.

11 The No 62 Mk II Set – this one is in a jeep – was developed at the end of the war, replacing the No 22 Set. It was also used by Airborne troops.

(All pics Royal Signals Museum except 7 Lt Dan Guravich/ Library and Archives Canada PA-146287)

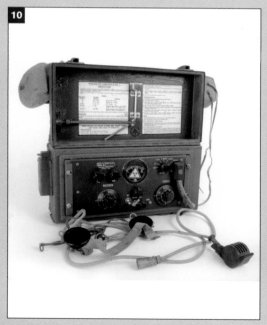

ABOVE An AEC 6 × 6 ACV, an improvement on the earlier Dorchesters, was used by the top commanders of armies and armoured divisions. *(Military Communications and Electronics Museum)*

BELOW As might be expected, many manufacturers made wireless lorries. This is a Leyland Retriever in the African desert in 1941. Others included the Bedford QLR which had special electrical equipment, an auxiliary generator driven by the transfer case power-take-off, various tent attachments and aerial fitment points. *(Royal Signals Museum)*

Signals vehicles

British Army signals vehicles during this period ranged from wireless lorries to armoured command vehicles (ACV). The first of the ACVs were 20 Guy Lizards built for the BEF in France. Guy couldn't produce sufficient, so AEC took over and built over 400 that were based on the AEC Matador chassis. They were nicknamed 'Dorchesters' after the palatial London hotel. The ACVs came into their own in the desert where both Montgomery and Rommel used them, the latter courtesy of two captured by Aufklärungsabteilung 3 in April 1941 along with two generals (Lts Gen Philip Neame and Richard O'Connor; a third general, Maj Gen Gambier-Parry escaped but lost his ACV). Rommel named his and that used by Gen Lt Ludwig Crüwell 'Max' and 'Moritz' after the Wilhelm Busch characters. The most impressive ACVs were the AEC 6 × 6s (over 150 built). Developed from the 'Dorchesters' they saw service in north-west Europe after D-Day.

There were many other command vehicles – in 21st Army Group these

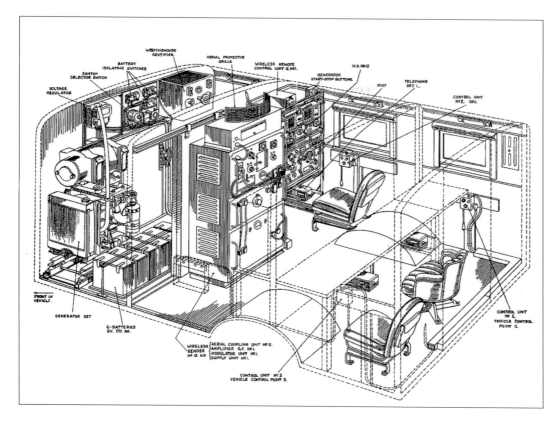

were based on the Bedford QL chassis designated QLR with electrical suppression. What they all had in common was that they accommodated staff officers as well as signallers – sometimes together, sometimes in separate compartments – with various wireless sets that communicated to their subordinates. Most would also have been able to communicate with higher commands. In addition, they would have short-range capabilities. Other signals lorries were also in abundance, wireless lorries providing communications at each level from army group and lines of communication through to armies, corps and divisions. Bedford QL/QLRs were the main chassis, as they were for the TEVs (terminal equipment vehicles that carried switchboards and teleprinters, with as many as 60 lines). There were also cable layers – although latterly Loyd or Universal

RIGHT The CMP 15cwt wireless truck was used by formations needing a No 19 set – mainly for communications with armoured units. (Library and Archives Canada/ecopy)

Carriers were used for this job. (Cable laying was additionally accomplished by land laying from a drum or from a smaller truck.)

The Bedford QL started quantity production in 1941 and over 52,000 had been built by 1945 in numerous variants. As well as the QLR there were the QLB, used as a Bofors gun tractor; QLC fire engine, which towed a trailer pump and carried an integral water tank, hoses and power take-off pump in the main body; it was also used as a fuel tanker with swinging booms to refuel aircraft; QLD general cargo truck; QLT troop transport – the 'Drooper' with a modified and lengthened chassis to accommodate the extra long body to carry 29 troops and kit – and the QLW tipper. It was powered by a 3.5-litre, six-cylinder petrol engine with a governed top speed of 38mph (61km/h). It had great mobility, a high ground clearance and a two-speed, four-wheel-drive transfer box located in the centre of the chassis that gave eight forward gear ratios. It was even used to portée the 6pdr anti-tank gun. The Royal Canadian Corps of Signals also provided a number of different vehicles: 3-ton lorries, 30cwt, 15cwt and 8cwt trucks, including the 'Gin Palace' – CMP Truck 15cwt Wireless – or Truck 8cwt Wireless.

ABOVE AND BELOW Signals communications during the Second World War involved line as much as radio, and that line – as in the First World War – often had to be laid and mended under fire. It was particularly important in defence, as was seen at Imphal and Kohima (above) and in the confines of the Normandy bridgehead (below). *(Both: Royal Signals Museum)*

BELOW Prinses Irene Brigade training with line in England. *(Nationaalarchief.nl)*

ABOVE The Royal Signals took over responsibility for the Carrier Pigeon Service in 1920. Some 32 messenger pigeons were awarded the Dickin Medal for gallantry. Perhaps the most famous use was at Arnhem when 'William of Orange' flew for 4hr 25min over 260 miles from Arnhem Bridge to its loft in Knutsford and told of the plight of the British Paras cut off at the bridge. *(Royal Signals Museum)*

BELOW Low tech they might be, and not too useful in low light conditions or poor terrain, but flags were used by both sides during the war. *(Royal Signals Museum)*

ABOVE An Australian signaller with a heliograph, which communicates by flashing reflected sunlight from its movable mirror. Heliographs have been around since the 1860s and have a remarkably long range.

Chapter Seven

Medical services

The Royal Army Medical Corps accompanied troops in every theatre. Medical advances helped ensure that the best possible facilities and treatment were available to the wounded. Penicillin was used for the first time in the North African campaign and blood transfusions became commonplace. With surgeons closer to the front line than ever before and improved casualty evacuation, even the huge variety of fighting environments proved no obstacle to better medical services.

OPPOSITE Based on the K30 light truck, the K2/Y 'Katy' was built by Austin with Mann-Egerton bodywork. Made famous by its starring role in the film *Ice Cold in Alex*, it was also the vehicle in which Queen Elizabeth II learnt to drive. *(Rob Mitchell/WikiCommons (CC0))*

The British Army has had a Royal Army Medical Corps since 1898 – but there had been considerable advances in technology when war broke out in 1939, providing better and quicker transport. By the end of the war, air evacuation meant that severely wounded casualties from north-west Europe could be in a hospital in Britain within hours. In Burma, where the distances could be much greater, air evacuation made a huge difference. The increase in the number and size of aircraft available meant that some 200,000 sick and wounded had been evacuated by air, with the loss of only one aircraft. The Allies' complete air superiority helped. Further medical developments – penicillin and blood transfusion to name but two – significantly improved casualty evacuation and treatment. However, no matter the technical advances, battlefield casualties had to be treated in battle conditions and that often took huge amounts of bravery from both medical staff and the stretcher-bearers.

The RAMC – as with so much of the post-First World War army – was starved of money and found recruitment difficult. However, the mid-1930s saw improvements following the publication of the second report by Warren Fisher (Permanent Secretary to the Treasury), which offered opportunities for promotion. The introduction of short-service commissions

helped, as did attempts to improve cooperation between medical officers and the fighting arms. All new entrants went to Boyce Barracks, Church Crookham, Hampshire – the corps training depot.

The Army School of Hygiene had looked carefully at energy output, calories and diet and was able to report in 1934 that recruits – often from poor areas of the community during the Depression – were gaining weight (average 9lb) during training at their depots, showing that the rations were working! There was also work done on washing military clothing – such a problem during the First World War. A new Army School of Hygiene was built in Keogh Barracks, Mytchett, Surrey. Courses were held there to instruct ORs in water supplies and sanitation in the field, and there were courses for officers who were likely to serve in tropical parts. (Today, the Museum of Army Medicine can be found here. One of the exhibits is L/Cpl Henry Harden RAMC's VC, won during Operation Blackcock while attached to 45 RM Cdo.)

British medical arrangements came to the fore in the Desert War where the Germans and Italians certainly came off second best to the British in standards of hygiene and sanitation, keeping sickness at bay. Much of the credit is directed at DMS Percy Tomlinson who was praised in particular by the Australians, not known for their tolerance of poor British medical facilities. This table, taken from Mark Harrison's *Medicine and Victory* sums it up well:

SICKNESS RATES IN THE BRITISH AND GERMAN ARMIES IN THE WESTERN DESERT (PER 1,000 MEN/MONTH)			
Months	**Year**	**German**	**British**
Oct–Dec	1941	154	52
Jan–Mar	1942	95	51
Apr–Jun	1942	105	42
July–Sept	1942	158	67
Oct–Dec	1942	153	52
Average		133	52

In Italy, the problem of malaria was solved by 1944 by heavy use of DDT, but that didn't work on the high incidence of VD, the highest recorded in any Second World War theatre. Penicillin helped keep manpower wastage levels low but it was apparent that appeals to discipline didn't work in Italy. In Burma,

RIGHT **This diagram shows the casualty extraction process from the front line to hospitals back in Britain. The Juno Centre, discussing casualties on its informative website, notes: 'The proportion of various casualties reported by No 15 Field Ambulance of 4th Canadian Armoured Division in September 1944 was representative of the Army as a whole: 10% of wounds were caused by rifles, 17.5% by machine guns, 14.5% by mortars, and almost 43% by artillery; about 27% of casualties had multiple wounds. Although these proportions would vary depending on the nature of the campaign being waged, artillery remained the main killer throughout the war.'** *(RCT/Eleanor Forty)*

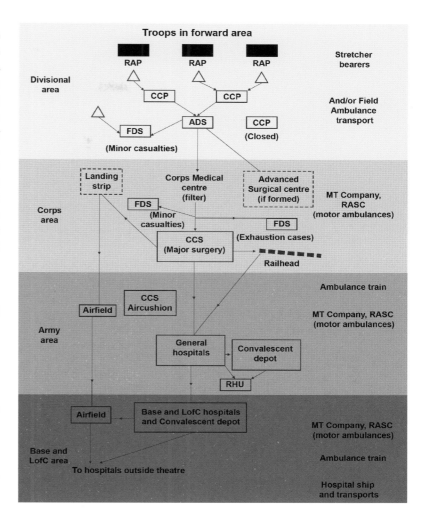

however, preventative medicine played a leading role which some – including the official medical historian, F.A.E. Crew – thought was crucial. Hospital admissions for sickness dropped from 1,850 per 1,000 troops per annum – *ie* nearly two bouts for each soldier – to 500, but Harrison points out that the key factor was the speed of recovery helped by the Corps Medical Centres that made a difference.

Casualty evacuation

In 1939 much of the RAMC's casualty evacuation system was based on that used in the First World War: from regimental aid post (RAP) to hospital in the UK. The system quickly proved unwieldy during the BEF's fighting in 1940 and changes had to be made. The Hartgill Committee was set up to examine the medical services in France and North Africa. The committee identified four main failures:

- the field units were too cumbersome and weren't mobile
- field ambulances didn't have suitable means of communications
- casualty evacuation was congested in forward areas, particularly when there was insufficient transport available
- surgeons were too far removed from the action.

Its proposed solutions were to ensure that triage/classification of the casualty happened as far forward as possible and that casualties

BELOW **A regimental aid post, this one of the 9th DLI after the battle for Lingèvres, during which the battalion took heavy casualties. These included its Commanding Officer, Colonel H. Woods, one of 33 from the DLI who died on 14 June 1944.**

ABOVE **Canadian combat medics construct a field hospital on Walcheren. The bad weather meant that many casualties had to wait for evacuation across the Scheldt. They were helped, as Terry Copp recalled, by the 'almost miraculous absence of abdominal wounds'. After five days an LCT came and was able to load all except a few cases before being forced to put to sea.** *(Provincial Archives of Alberta/Flickr Commons)*

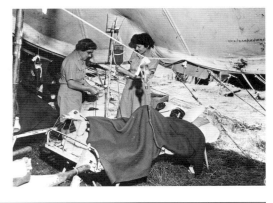

RIGHT AND BELOW
Suggested layout of a surgical block of a CCS.
(RCT)

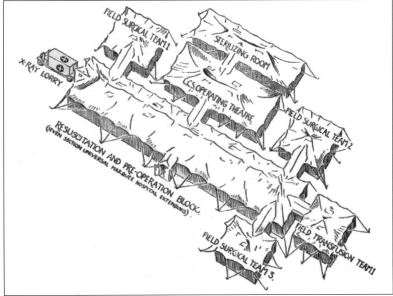

would be taken directly to the medical unit that would best serve them. It also proposed the creation of new units: such as the field dressing station (FDS) and field surgical unit (FSU).

The new system was difficult to put in place in 1943 and only 21st Army Group would benefit from its changes. As Harrison reported:

these new arrangements stood the test: thousands of men received closure of their wounds within three to five days of wounding, as opposed to an average of ten to fourteen days in previous campaigns, and with a success rate of nearly 95 percent after the bridgehead had been successfully established. This meant that a man with a flesh wound was normally returned to duty within six weeks.

The casualty evacuation route started, as it always had done, with regimental collection and initial treatment before being moved to the advanced dressing station (ADS), now closer to the front line. Here, a much more detailed sorting process saw casualties divided into groups:

1. Casualty in shock and needing resuscitation/transfusion. These went straight to a FDS (there were usually two for an infantry division) which usually had a field transfusion unit (FTU) nearby. The British Army was the only army to enter the war with an established transfusion service.
2. Casualties needing immediate surgical attention went to the advanced surgical centre (ASC), which was made up of the Corps FDS with a FSU and FTU.
3. The rest were to go to the casualty clearing station (CCS). This needed to be kept small and mobile, and was restricted to 50 beds/70 stretcher cases. It was still dependent on the RASC for transport (integral transport being refused by the War Office).

Flexibility was important and was needed when contemplating the assault on the Atlantic Wall where heavy casualties were expected. The decision was taken to provide an FDS/FSU within the Beach Group and evacuate the casualties over the beach on dedicated vessels that would take them to hospitals in Portsmouth

and Southampton readied for the task. Air evacuation from Normandy was also important, starting earlier than anticipated on 13 June. Flexibility was also important in Burma where the front lines were not fixed and evacuation convoys had to be protected. Jungle Surgical Units were developed to allow man-portability. Airborne troops, too, need flexible medical services. Airborne medical staff were trained to be able to treat casualties and hold them until they could link up with ground forces.

Battalion medical units

All soldiers carried a field dressing for immediate use; there was even a specific pocket for it in the battledress. Many also carried a bandage in the scrim covering of their helmets, although this was more prevalent in the US Army. All soldiers were trained in simple first aid, including the use of morphine.

The basic arrangement for the treatment of casualties started with the battalion who had a Medical Officer – a captain, a qualified doctor, many with surgical skills. The MO was supported by an RAMC Medical Orderly and a Medical Sergeant. The MO set up a RAP just behind the front line. Walking wounded or casualties collected by the stretcher-bearers (each battalion had 20–22 men trained by the MO, the Regimental Band if there was one). They had a 15cwt truck in which to carry their equipment.

From the RAP the Field Ambulance (an HQ and two companies) provided stretcher units

ABOVE LEFT Much of the casualty evacuation of stretcher-borne casualties was effected by jeeps. Here a casualty is loaded into a Willys MB ambulance jeep in Sonsbeck, Germany, 6 March 1945. *(Capt Jack H. Smith/Library and Archives Canada PA-113872)*

ABOVE On Walcheren Alligators were pressed into service for casualty evacuation. *(Provincial Archives of Alberta/Flickr Commons)*

FAR LEFT Medical staff in north-west Europe treated the wounded of both sides.

LEFT An unusual jungle casevac for this casualty in the Arakan.

RIGHT All soldiers were taught first aid. This leaflet was one of the resources provided (in this case to all ranks down to and including corporals). *(RCT)*

FAR RIGHT A medical orderly with a double-size water bottle. He has three long-service chevrons (in red pointing up) on his lower right sleeve. He carries medical gear in his pouches and small pack which is marked with a red cross. They contain such items as cotton wool, gauze, bandages, zinc oxide plaster, a sulphanilamide dredger, morphine ampoules and various tablets – aspirin, caffeine, phenacetin, and so on.

RIGHT A 51st Highland Division medical orderly. Note the Black Watch tartan insignia below the three red arm-of-service infantry lines – these denote the third, or junior, brigade in the division – in 1944 the 154th Inf Bde.

RIGHT Morale-boosting visits by top brass were all well and good, but when you're fighting for king and country, it's quite good to see the man himself: King George VI is seen here on a visit to North Africa in June 1943.

to take the wounded to an ADS or direct to the main dressing station (MDS). The onward path is shown in the diagram on page 157.

Medical services included more than dealing with battle casualties. Sanitation, prevention of disease – from malaria to VD – mental breakdown: six years of war affected mind and body. Few men could endure the continued atrocity of war and unsurprisingly, perhaps, it became clear that most broke down after 200–240 days in combat. Spotting the signs and taking remedial action was important. While the British Army no longer shot deserters, unlike their opponents, the military establishment was obviously concerned at the high levels of desertion seen in Italy after bad weather and heavy fighting. Tracy Craggs touches on this in her PhD dissertation in relation to the 2/EYorks – that 3rd Division recorded high proportions of battle exhaustion as compared to wounded after the fighting around the Maas. She quotes a monthly medical bulletin that blamed 'cold and wet weather, inability to dig proper slit trenches due to the waterlogged ground; a prolonged battle with not very much progress and the continual fear of mines'. The bulletin notes that exhaustion, affected by lowered morale caused by the number of casualties, played a big part. In November 1944 the division ensured that an MO assessed new cases at the ADS and winnowed out those who needed more careful treatment. Certainly, officers were told to ensure they did as much as possible to help morale.

AMBULANCE

Austin K2/Y Ambulance

Manufacturers: Austin and Mann Egerton
(United Kingdom)
Number produced: 13,102
Weight: 3.1 tons (3,124kg) (dry)
Overall length: 18ft (5.49m)
Width: 7ft 5in (2.26m)
Height: 9ft 2in (2.79m)
Crew: 2–3
Engine: 3.5-litre Austin 6-cylinder
Transmission: 4 forward, 1 reverse
Layout: Four wheels, two driven
Payload: 4 stretchers or 10 passengers
Fuel capacity: 24gal (109 litres)
Top speed: 50mph (80km/h)

The Austin K2/Y ambulance – nicknamed
'Katy' – was part of the everyday scenery
to Allied infantrymen as over 13,000
were supplied to British, Commonwealth
and American forces throughout the war.
It was manufactured at the Longbridge
factory and, being directly derived from the
Austin K30 commercial truck, little extra
development work was needed, the most
significant change being that it featured
canvas doors. The bodywork was provided
by Mann Egerton to a Royal Army Medical
Corps design. This had two large rear
doors, with a third internal door between
the cab and the rear. It was intended
to take ten sitting casualties or four on
stretchers; however, in extremis many
more could be carried.

The ambulance featured a six-cylinder
3.5-litre Austin petrol engine and a four-
speed transmission – these gave it a top
speed of about 50mph (80km/h). It had
a fuel tank on each side, together giving a
capacity of around 24gal (109 litres). Two
different variants were manufactured – the
earliest had circular ventilation intakes on
the roof and a large humped cover over
the spare wheel. The later one had fixed
square ventilators and a smaller wheel
cover, intended to help reduce accidental
collisions with other vehicles.

ABOVE AND LEFT
Exterior and interior
of an Austin K2/Y.
Katies could take
ten casualties or
four stretcher cases,
although there are
stories of considerably
larger numbers
travelling in extremis.
(Alec Small)

LEFT AND BELOW
A pair of publicity
photographs showing
a Katy delivering
casualties by stretcher
to a FDS in Libya.
In 1941–42 the
next step would be
transferral to a CCS,
for surgery and short-
term convalescence.
However, by 1944
and the invasion
of Normandy, the
system had changed
and in order to get
the wounded into
surgery faster, FDSs
had been combined
with transfusion and
surgical units to form
advanced surgical
centres that worked
closer to the front lines.

Chapter Eight

Remembrance

━━━(●)━━━━━━━━━━━━━━━━━━

**Care of the dead is important
not only to the bereaved
families but to all soldiers. The
Commonwealth War Graves
Commission (CWGC) was set
up after the First World War
to ensure that all should be
commemorated equally and,
recently, has taken steps to
rectify the mistakes of the
past that allowed many of the
burials of colonial troops to go
unrecorded. There are now
over 23,000 CWGC sites around
the world.**

**OPPOSITE The CWGC Reichswald Forest War Cemetery,
designed by Philip Hepworth, is the largest Commonwealth
cemetery in Germany. Burials from all over the country were
brought here at the end of the war; today, there are 7,594
Commonwealth servicemen buried or commemorated and 78
of other nationalities including Polish and Czech. This group of
graves are men of the 2nd Battalion, The Gordon Highlanders
who fell on 24 March 1945 as they took part in the crossing of the
Rhine at Xanten as part of operation Torchlight.**

ABOVE Soldiers from 8th/9th Battalion, the Royal Australian Regiment, during a memorial service with the Royal Thai Armed Forces at Hellfire Pass. It was the longest and deepest cutting of the Burma Railway and symbolises the suffering and maltreatment of Australian prisoners in the Asia-Pacific region in the Second World War. (© Commonwealth of Australia, Department of Defence)

ABOVE One of many memorials in Europe to infantry regiments, this one remembers the fallen of the 4th and 5th Battalions of the Wiltshire Regiment who died between 22 September and 6 October 1944 during the Battle for the Island and the relief of the paras at Arnhem.

British and Commonwealth infantrymen and the part they played in the Second World War are remembered all around the globe in the form of national memorials, battle memorials and, of course, cemeteries. Set up in 1917 as the Imperial War Graves Commission – and renamed the Commonwealth War Graves Commission (CWGC) in 1960 – the member states (Australia, Canada, India, New Zealand, South Africa and the UK) agreed core principles identified on the excellent CWGC website:

- Each of the Commonwealth dead should be commemorated by name on a headstone or memorial
- Headstones and memorials should be permanent
- Headstones should be uniform
- There should be equality of treatment for the war dead irrespective of rank or religion.

There are 23,000 CWGC memorials and cemeteries at 150 locations, remembering those whose burial locations are known and the thousands of missing.

Anyone who has visited a CWGC cemetery will know just how well appointed and cared for they are. Carefully and thoughtfully designed by such luminaries as Sir Edwin Lutyens, Sir Herbert Baker and Sir

BELOW The liberation of the town of Best by the 15th Scottish Division is remembered by this distinctive sculpture of three Scotsmen jumping through tartan.

Reginald Blomfield (the latter designing the Cross of Sacrifice that can be found at all CWGC cemeteries containing 40 or more graves) – with literary advice from Rudyard Kipling – the catalyst for their creation was Sir Fabian Ware.

By 1939, the commission had the infrastructure and locations remembering the First World War but had to build anew to commemorate the fallen of 1939–45. Around 581,000 servicemen and women who died in the Second World War are remembered.

Perhaps the most obvious memorial in Britain is the Cenotaph on Whitehall in London, designed by Lutyens, around which the annual Service of Remembrance is focused. While the most massive memorials – Thiepval on the Somme, Tyne Cot and the Menin Gate around Ypres, the Canadian memorial at Vimy Ridge – remember the fallen of the First World War, the infantrymen of the Second World War are remembered at significant sites such as the Alamein Memorial in Egypt, unveiled by Viscount Montgomery of Alamein in 1953, the Price of Peace Memorial in Ortona, Italy, the numerous memorials in Normandy and north-west Europe, the Australian War Memorial in Canberra and many, many more. Unfortunately, however, there is currently no memorial dedicated to those of the Indian Army who fell: caught up in the politics of empire, their huge contribution is remembered in memorials at CWGC cemeteries at Kohima and Imphal, Singapore and Jakarta, Tehran and Cassino, among many others.

ABOVE LEFT British 3rd Infantry Division's insignia stands outside the rebuilt castle walls of Caen, the scene of such protracted fighting in June and July 1944.

ABOVE Canadian artist Colin Gibson sculpted 'Remembrance and Renewal', which stands outside the Juno Beach Centre in Normandy.

ABOVE Inaugurated by the wartime commander of Fourteenth Army, Gen Sir William Slim, the Kohima War Cemetery is famous for two memorials: to Indian and Sikh soldiers and to 2nd Infantry Division on which is incised the Kohima Epitaph – 'When you go home tell them of us and say for your tomorrow we gave our today'. *(Isaxar/ WikiCommons (CC BY-SA 4.0))*

BELOW On the road between Caen and Falaise there are two big cemeteries: that of the 1st Polish Armoured Division at Grainville-Langannerie and the Bretteville-sur-Laize Canadian War Cemetery (here). Many of these burials are from the fighting to close the Falaise Gap and the last days of the Allies' great victory in Normandy. The Poles fought with First Canadian Army as part of 21st (BR) Army Group.

Abbreviations and glossary

(For regimental abbreviations see pages 32–33)

2AIF	2nd Australian Imperial Force
2IC	Second in command
9/The Loyal Regt	9th Battalion, The Loyal Regiment
ACC	Army Catering Corps
ACV	Armoured command vehicle
AGRA	Army Group RA. Army troops usually assigned to corps. Normally composed of five or six regiments, a heavy and various medium
AP	Armour-piercing
APC	Armoured personnel carrier
APCBC	Armour-piercing, capped, ballistic cap
APCR	Armour-piercing, composite rigid
APDS	Armour-piercing, discarding sabot
ATk	Anti-tank
Barrage	Fire directed in moving belts. A creeping barrage provides a moving line of fire in front of advancing troops to neutralise and suppress defenders. A lifting barrage fires on an enemy line, lifting as friendly troops arrive
BD	Battledress. Introduced in 1939, British battledress was worn by many of the combatants of the Second World War – particularly British Dominions and Commonwealth and others who fought with them (Poles, Free French before they were equipped by the United States). BD might not have looked good but it was carefully designed
BEF	British Expeditionary Force – the British forces sent to France in 1939–40
BLA	British Liberation Army – the British forces in north-west Europe that became British Army of the Rhine in August 1945
Bombardment	A planned engagement of a target or targets over a period of time (sometimes days). Pre-attack bombardments are supposed to soften up the enemy, damaging defences and troops' morale. Their success depended mainly on how well dug in the enemy forces were
Brigade	The smallest formation in the British Army. Everything smaller than a brigade is a unit; brigades and above are formations.
Burma	Today's Myanmar. Burma was a British colony in the 19th century, gaining independence on 4 January 1948
Calibre (cal)	The diameter of the bore of a gun barrel. Also used as a unit of length of a gun barrel. For example a 10in/20cal gun would have a barrel 200 inches long (10 × 20).This is specified in millimetres, centimetres or inches, depending on the historical period and national preference

Canloan	In autumn 1943 Canada had a surplus of junior officers. The opportunity to serve with the British Army was offered and, in the case of 623 infantry and 50 ordnance officers, taken up. The Canloan officers served with distinction with a remarkable 75% ending up as casualties: 128 died, 310 were wounded and 27 were made PoWs. These were gallant men who served their country and the British Army well
CCS	Casualty clearing station
CMF	Central Mediterranean Forces
CMP	Canadian Military Pattern or Corps of Military Police
CO	Commanding officer
Commonwealth	Created in 1926 and formally constituted in 1949, Britain and its Dominions – Australia, New Zealand, Canada and Newfoundland – agreed they were 'equal in status, in no way subordinate one to another in any aspect of their domestic or external affairs, though united by common allegiance to the Crown, and freely associated as members of the British Commonwealth of Nations'. This changed in 1949 when new criteria were set up not relevant to this book
Concentration	When more than one battery fires at the same target area
Counter-battery	Developed during the First World War, CB fire was mainly effected through careful observation from air and land, flash-spotting, sound-ranging, wireless/radio intercepts, prisoner interrogation and patrolling. Only late in the war did radar come in. Each corps had a counter-battery officer (CBO) and staff
Covering fire	Supporting friendly operations with planned barrages or time concentrations
CRSigs	Commander Royal Signals
CSM	Company Sergeant Major
CWGC	Commonwealth War Graves Commission
cwt	hundredweight = 112lb (US 100lb)
Defensive fire	Pre-planned fire to protect against an enemy attack
Direct fire	Aiming and firing at targets visible from the weapon – essential for ATk guns
DR	Dispatch rider
FAT	Field artillery tractor
FBE	Folding boat equipment
FOO	Forward observation officer
FSR	Field Service Regulations